"To Papa on his
Birthday – "60"th
Love from
Pammy "29"th
Sept. 1978
Love from
Alan & Elsie

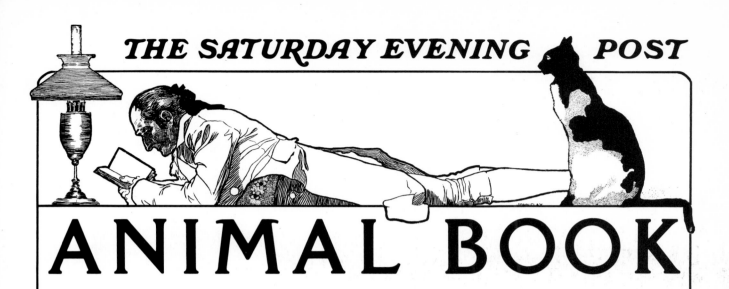

THE SATURDAY EVENING POST

ANIMAL BOOK

THE SATURDAY EVENING POST
ANIMAL BOOK

Fiction, fact and fantasy about the birds and
the beasts, with illustrations from
The Saturday Evening Post

THE CURTIS PUBLISHING COMPANY
Indianapolis, Indiana

The Saturday Evening Post Animal Book

Jean White, Editor

Sandra Strother-Young, Art Director and Designer

Starkey Flythe, Jr., Editorial Director, Curtis
Book Division

Jack Merritt, President, Curtis Book Division

David M. Price, Production Manager, Curtis
Book Division

Art Staff: Lucian Lupinski, Jinny Sauer,
Kathleen Saunders

Compositors: Marie Caldwell, Gloria McCoy,
Penny Allison, Geri Watson, Rose Thompson

Production Assistants: Marianne Roan, Dwight Lamb

Editorial Staff: Louise Fortson, Michael Morris, John J.
Rea, John D. Craton and Astrid Henkels, a good friend and
valued associate who is not with us to see this
book completed.

The stream, the swamp, the river, the mountain. . . . A century hence they will not be here as I see them. Nature will have been robbed of many brilliant charms, the rivers will be tormented and turned astray from their primitive courses, the hills will be levelled with the swamps. Scarce a magnolia will Louisiana possess, the timid deer will exist nowhere, fish will no longer abound in the rivers, the eagle will scarce ever alight.

John James Audubon

All things bright and beautiful,
  All creatures great and small,
  All things wise and wonderful,
    The Lord God made them all.

Cecil Francis Alexander

The beauty and genius of a work of art may be reconceived, though its first material expression be destroyed; a vanished harmony may yet again inspire the composer; but when the last individual of a race of living things breathes no more, another heaven and another earth must pass before such a one can be again.

William Beebe

We ought to investigate all sorts of animals because all of them will reveal something of nature and something of beauty.

Aristotle

Tyger, tyger: burning bright
In the forests of the night,
What immortal hand or eye
Could frame thy fearful symmetry?

William Blake

I never saw a wild thing
Sorry for itself.

D. H. Lawrence

We need another and a wiser and perhaps a more mystical concept of animals. Remote from universal nature, and living by complicated artifice, man in civilization surveys the creature through the glass of his knowledge and sees thereby a feather magnified and the whole image in distortion. We patronize them for their incompleteness, for their tragic fate of having taken form so far below ourselves. And therein we err, and greatly err. For the animal shall not be measured by man. In a world older and more complete than ours they move finished and complete, gifted with extensions of the senses we have lost or never attained, living by voices we shall never hear. They are not brethren, they are not underlings; they are other nations, caught with ourselves in the net of life and time, fellow prisoners of the splendour and travail of the earth.

Henry Beston, *The Outermost House*

CONTENTS

ANIMALS WHO CAME IN FROM THE COLD

The first of them joined man at his fireside some 40,000 years ago, exchanging independence for warmth, food and companionship. These animals are our allies, our associates, our friends—they are our pets.

LIFE WITH THE ANIMALS

True tales of personal experiences with animals, large and small, under a variety of circumstances.

THE HUNTER AND HUNTED

THE CALL OF THE WILD

by Jack London

"Old longings nomadic leap,
Chafing at custom's chain;
Again from its brumal sleep
Wakens the ferine strain."

CHARLES LIVINGSTON BULL

The hero of this short novel is a huge and very intelligent dog, half St. Bernard and half shepherd, named Buck. When the story begins in 1897, Buck is a kindly treated pet on a California ranch. Then his world changes. In Jack London's words:

"Buck did not read the newspapers, or he would have known that trouble was brewing, not alone for himself, but for every tidewater dog, strong of muscle and with warm long hair, from Puget Sound to San Diego. Because men, groping in the Arctic darkness, had found a yellow metal, and because steamship and transportation companies were booming the find, thousands of men were rushing into the Northland. These men wanted dogs . . ."

Buck is stolen and shipped to Alaska where men are outfitting for the last great gold rush to the Klondike, and he is sold as a sled dog. Cruelly beaten by men who try to break his spirit, Buck sheds the habits of civilization. He learns to obey his new owners out of respect for their clubs and whips; he learns to sleep burrowed in a snowbank for warmth, and to fight the other dogs for the extra mouthful of food that will help him survive. And, in the smoke of wilderness campfires, Buck begins to see visions of an older world where dog-wolves are the hunting companions of shaggy-haired primitive men. He begins to hear in the Arctic night a call that sets his blood racing.

Overworked and underfed, Buck is near death when he is rescued from cruel and stupid owners by prospector John Thornton. His strength returns, and he is free at last to explore the wilderness.

Spring came on once more, and at the end of all their wandering they found, not the Lost Cabin, but a shallow placer in a broad valley where the gold showed like yellow butter across the bottom of the washing-pan. They sought no farther. Each day they worked earned them thousands of dollars in clean dust and nuggets, and they worked every day. The gold was sacked in moose-hide bags, fifty pounds to the bag, and piled like so much firewood outside the spruce-bough lodge. Like giants they toiled, days flashing on the heels of days like dreams as they heaped the treasure up.

There was nothing for the dogs to do, save the hauling in of meat now and again that Thornton killed, and Buck spent long hours musing by the fire. The vision of the short-legged hairy man came to him more frequently, now that there was little work to be done; and often, blinking by the fire, Buck wandered with him in that other world which he remembered.

The salient thing of this other world seemed fear. When he watched the hairy man sleeping by the fire, head between his knees and hands clasped above, Buck saw that he slept restlessly, with many starts and awakenings, at which times he would peer fearfully into the darkness and fling more

"The greatest dog story of all time," critics have called this masterpiece of action and adventure writing. It first appeared as a serial in The Saturday Evening Post *in 1903 with illustrations by Charles Livingston Bull.*

wood upon the fire. Did they walk by the beach of a sea, where the hairy man gathered shellfish and ate them as he gathered, it was with eyes that roved everywhere for hidden danger and with legs prepared to run like the wind at its first appearance. Through the forest they crept noiselessly, Buck at the hairy man's heels; and they were alert and vigilant, the pair of them, ears twitching and moving and nostrils quivering, for the man heard and smelled as keenly as Buck. The hairy man could spring up into the trees and travel ahead as fast as on the ground, swinging by the arms from limb to limb, sometimes a dozen feet apart, letting go and catching, never falling, never missing his grip. In fact, he seemed as much at home among the trees as on the ground; and Buck had memories of nights of

vigil spent beneath trees wherein the hairy man roosted, holding on tightly as he slept.

And closely akin to the visions of the hairy man was the call still sounding in the depths of the forest. It filled him with a great unrest and strange desires. It caused him to feel a vague, sweet gladness, and he was aware of wild yearnings and stirrings for he knew not what. Sometimes he pursued the call into the forest, looking for it as though it were a tangible thing, barking softly or defiantly, as the mood might dictate. He would thrust his nose into the cool wood moss, or into the black soil where long grasses grew, and snort with joy at the fat earth smells; or he would crouch for hours, as if in concealment, behind fungus-covered trunks of fallen trees, wide-eyed and wide-eared to all that moved and sounded about him. It might be, lying thus, that he hoped to surprise this call he could not understand. But he did not know why he did these various things. He was impelled to do them, and did not reason about the things he did at all.

Irresistible impulses seized him. He would be lying in camp, dozing lazily in the heat of the day, when suddenly his head would lift and his ears cock up, intent and listening, and he would spring to his feet and dash away, and on and on, for hours, through the forest aisles and across the open spaces where the niggerheads bunched. He loved to run down dry watercourses, and to creep and spy upon the bird life in the woods. For a day at a time he would lie in the underbrush where he could watch the partridges drumming and strutting up and down. But especially he loved to run in the dim twilight of the summer midnights, listening to the subdued and sleepy murmurs of the forest, reading signs and sounds as man may read a book, and seeking for the mysterious something that called—called, waking or sleeping, at all times, for him to come.

One night he sprang from sleep with a start, eager-eyed, nostrils quivering and scenting, his mane bristling in recurrent waves. From the forest came the call (or one note of it, for the call was many-noted), distinct and definite as never before—a long-drawn howl, like, yet unlike, any noise made by husky dog. And he knew it, in the old familiar way, as a sound heard before. He sprang through the sleeping camp and in swift silence dashed through the woods. As he drew closer to the cry he went more slowly, with caution

"He would spring to his feet and dash away, on and on for hours, through the forest aisles and open spaces."

in every movement, till he came to an open place among the trees, and looking out saw, erect on haunches, with nose pointed to the sky, a long, lean, timber wolf.

He had made no noise, yet it ceased from its howling and tried to sense his presence. Buck stalked out into the open, half crouching, body gathered compactly together, tail straight and stiff, feet falling with unwonted care. Every movement advertised commingled threatening and overture of friendliness. It was the menacing truce that marks the meeting of wild beasts that prey. But the wolf fled at sight of him. He followed, with wild leapings, in a frenzy to overtake. He ran him into a blind channel, in the bed of the creek, where a timber jam barred the way. The wolf whirled about, pivoting on his hind legs after the fashion of Joe and of all cornered husky dogs, snarling, his hair bristling, clipping his teeth together in a continuous and rapid succession of snaps.

Buck did not attack, but circled him about and hedged him in with friendly advances. The wolf was suspicious and afraid; for Buck made three of him in weight, while his head barely reached to Buck's shoulder. Watching his chance, he darted away, and the chase was resumed. Time and again he was cornered and the thing repeated, though he was in poor condition or Buck could not so easily have overtaken him. He would run till Buck's head was even with his flank, when he would whirl around at bay, only to dash away again at the first opportunity.

But in the end Buck's pertinacity was rewarded; for the wolf, finding that no harm was intended,

4

finally sniffed noses with him. Then they became friendly, and played about in the nervous, half-coy way with which fierce beasts belie their fierceness. After some time of this the wolf started off at an easy lope in a manner that plainly showed he was going somewhere. He made it clear to Buck that he was to come, and they ran side by side through the somber twilight, straight up the creek bed, into the gorge from which it issued, and across the bleak divide where it took its rise.

On the opposite slope of the watershed they came down into a level country where were great stretches of forest and many streams, and through these great stretches they ran steadily, hour after hour, the sun rising higher and the day growing ever warmer. Buck was wildly glad. He knew he was at last answering the call, running by the side of his wood brother toward the place from where the call surely came. Old memories were coming upon him fast, and he was stirring to them as of old he stirred to the realities of which they were the shadows. He had done this thing before, somewhere in that other

"Behind him were the shades of all manner of dogs, half-dogs and wild wolves, dreaming with him and becoming themselves the stuff of his dreams."

and dimly remembered world, and he was doing it again, now, running free in the open, the unpacked earth underfoot, the wide sky overhead.

They stopped by a running stream to drink, and, stopping, Buck remembered John Thornton. He sat down. The wolf started on toward the place from where the call surely came, then returned to him, sniffing noses and making actions as though to encourage him. But Buck turned about and started slowly on the back track. For the better part of an hour the wild brother ran by his side, whining softly. Then he sat down, pointed his nose upward, and howled. It was a mournful howl, and as Buck held steadily on his way he heard it grow faint and fainter until it was lost in the distance.

John Thornton was eating dinner when Buck dashed into camp and sprang upon him in a frenzy of affection, overturning him, scrambling upon

him, licking his face, biting his hand—"playing the general tom-fool," as John Thornton characterized it, the while he shook Buck back and forth and cursed him lovingly.

For two days and nights Buck never left camp, never let Thornton out of his sight. He followed him about at his work, watched him while he ate, saw him into his blankets at night and out of them in the morning. But after two days the call in the forest began to sound more imperiously than ever. Buck's restlessness came back on him, and he was haunted by recollections of the wild brother, and of the smiling land beyond the divide and the run side by side through the wide forest stretches. Once again he took to wandering in the woods, but the wild brother came no more; and though he listened through many a long vigil, the mournful howl was never raised.

He began to sleep out at night, staying away from camp for days at a time; and once he crossed the divide at the head of the creek and went down into the land of timber and of streams. There he wandered for over a week, seeking vainly for fresh sign of the wild brother, killing his meat as he traveled and traveling with the long, easy lope that seems never to tire. He fished for salmon in a broad stream that emptied somewhere into the sea, and by this stream he killed a large black bear, blinded by the mosquitoes while likewise fishing, and raging through the forest helpless and terrible. Even so, it was a hard fight, and it aroused the last latent remnants of Buck's ferocity. And two days later, when he returned to his kill and found a dozen wolverines quarreling over the spoil, he scattered them like chaff; and those that fled left two behind who would quarrel no more.

The blood-longing became stronger than ever before. He was a killer, a thing that preyed, living on the things that lived, unaided, alone, by virtue of his own strength and prowess, surviving triumphantly in a hostile environment where only the strong survived. Because of all this he became possessed of a great pride in himself, which communicated itself like a contagion to his physical being. It advertised itself in all his movements, was apparent in the play of every muscle, spoke plainly as speech in the way he carried himself, and made his glorious furry coat if anything more glorious. But for the stray brown on his muzzle and above his eyes, and for the splash of white hair that ran midmost down his chest, he might well have been mistaken for a gigantic wolf, larger than the largest of the breed. From his St. Bernard father he had inherited size and weight, but it was his shepherd mother who had given shape to that size and weight. His muzzle was the long wolf muzzle, save that it was larger than the muzzle of any wolf; and his head, somewhat broader, was the wolf head on a more massive scale.

His cunning was wolf cunning, and wild cunning; his intelligence, shepherd intelligence and St. Bernard intelligence; and all this, plus an experience gained in the fiercest of schools, made him as formidable a creature as any that roamed the wild. A carnivorous animal, living on a straight meat diet, he was in full flower, at the high tide of his life, overspilling with vigor and virility. When Thornton passed a caressing hand along his back, a snapping and crackling followed the hand, each hair discharging its pent magnetism at the contact. Every part, brain and body, nerve tissue and fiber, was keyed to the most exquisite pitch; and between all the parts there was a perfect equilibrium or adjustment. To sights and sounds and events which required action, he responded with lightning-like rapidity. Quickly as a husky dog could leap to defend from attack or to attack, he could leap twice as quickly. He saw the movement, or heard sound, and responded in less time than another dog required to compass the mere seeing or hearing. He perceived and determined and responded in the same instant. In point of fact the three actions of perceiving, determining, and responding were sequential; but so infinitesimal were the intervals of time between them that they appeared simultaneous. His muscles were surcharged with vitality, and snapped into play sharply, like steel springs. Life streamed through him in splendid flood, glad and rampant, until it seemed that it would burst him asunder in sheer ecstasy and pour forth generously over the world.

"Never was there such a dog," said John Thornton one day, as the partners watched Buck marching out of camp.

"When he was made, the mold was broke."

"Py jingo! I t'ink so mineself," Hans affirmed.

They saw him marching out of camp, but they did not see the instant and terrible transformation which took place as soon as he was within the secrecy of the forest. He no longer marched. At once he became a thing of the wild, stealing along softly, cat-footed, a passing shadow that appeared and disappeared among the shadows. He knew how to take advantage of every cover, to crawl on his belly like a snake, and like a snake to leap and strike. He could take a ptarmigan from its nest, kill a rabbit as it slept, and snap in mid air the little chipmunks fleeing a second too late for the trees. Fish, in open pools, were not too quick for him; nor were beaver, mending their dams, too wary. He killed to eat, not from wantonness; but he preferred to eat what he killed himself. So a lurking humor ran through his deeds, and it was his delight to steal upon the squirrels, and, when he all but had them, to let them go, chattering in mortal fear to the treetops.

As the fall of the year came on, the moose appeared in greater abundance, moving slowly down to meet the winter in the lower and less rigorous valleys. Buck had already dragged down a stray part-grown calf, but he wished strongly for larger and more formidable quarry, and he came upon it one day on the divide at the head of the creek. A band of twenty moose had crossed over from the land of streams and timber, and chief among them was a great bull. He was in a savage temper, and, standing over six feet from the ground, was as formidable an antagonist as ever Buck could desire. Back and forth the bull tossed his great palmated antlers, branching to fourteen points and embracing seven feet within the tips. His small eyes burned with a vicious and bitter light, while he roared with fury at sight of Buck.

From the bull's side, just forward of the flank, protruded a feathered arrow-end, which accounted for his savageness. Guided by that instinct which came from the old hunting days of the primordial world, Buck proceeded to cut the bull out from the herd. It was no slight task. He would bark and dance about in front of the bull, just out of reach of the great antlers and of the terrible splay hoofs which could have stamped his life out with a single blow. Unable to turn his back on the fanged danger and go on, the bull would be driven into paroxysms of rage. At such moments he charged Buck, who retreated craftily, luring him on by a simulated inability to escape. But when he was thus separated

"He killed a large black bear, blinded by mosquitoes while fishing, . . . raging through the forest, helpless and terrible."

from his fellows, two or three of the younger bulls would charge back upon Buck and enable the wounded bull to rejoin the herd.

There is a patience of the wild—dogged, tireless, persistent as life itself—that holds motionless for endless hours the spider in its web, the snake in its coils, the panther in its ambuscade; this patience belongs peculiarly to life when it hunts its living food; and it belonged to Buck as he clung to the flank of the herd, retarding its march, irritating the young bulls, worrying the cows with their half-grown calves, and driving the wounded bull mad with helpless rage. For half a day this continued. Buck multiplied himself, attacking from all sides,

enveloping the herd in a whirlwind of menace, cutting out his victim as fast as it could rejoin its mates, wearing out the patience of creatures preyed upon, which is a lesser patience than that of creatures preying.

As the day wore along and the sun dropped to its bed in the northwest (the darkness had come back and the fall nights were six hours long), the young bulls retraced their steps more and more reluctantly to the aid of their beset leader. The down-coming winter was harrying them on to the lower levels, and it seemed they could never shake off this tireless creature that held them back. Besides, it was not the life of the herd, or of the young bulls,

7

"In the fall of the year, the moose appeared in greater abundance, moving down to meet the winter in the lower valleys."

that was threatened. The life of only one member was demanded, which was a remoter interest than their lives, and in the end they were content to pay the toll.

As twilight fell the old bull stood with lowered head, watching his mates—the cows he had known, the calves he had fathered, the bulls he had mastered—as they shambled on at a rapid pace through the fading light. He could not follow, for before his nose leaped the merciless fanged terror that would not let him go. Three hundred pounds more than half a ton he weighed; he had lived a long, strong life, full of fight and struggle, and at the end he faced death at the teeth of a creature whose head did not reach beyond his great knuckled knees.

From then on, night and day, Buck never left his prey, never gave it a moment's rest, never permitted it to browse the leaves of trees or the shoots of young birch and willow. Nor did he give the wounded bull opportunity to slake his burning thirst in the slender trickling streams they crossed. Often, in desperation, he burst into long stretches of flight. At such times Buck did not attempt to stay him, but loped easily at his heels, satisfied with the way the game was played, lying down when the moose stood still, attacking him fiercely when he strove to eat or drink.

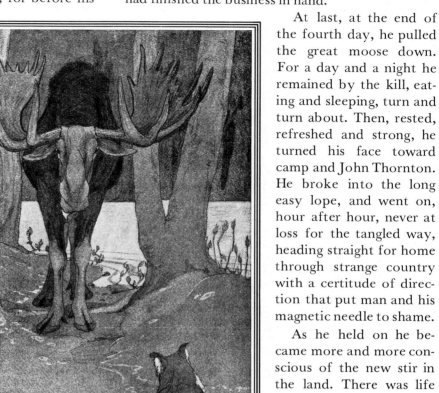

"The great head drooped more under its tree of horns."

The great head drooped more and more under its trees of horns, and the shambling trot grew weaker and weaker. He took to standing for long periods, with nose to the ground and dejected ears dropped limply; and Buck found more time in which to get water for himself and in which to rest. At such moments, panting with red lolling tongue and with eyes fixed upon the big bull, it appeared to Buck that a change was coming over the face of things. He could feel a new stir in the land. As the moose were coming into the land, other kinds of life were coming in. Forest and stream and air seemed palpitant with their presence. The news of it was borne in upon him, not by sight or sound, or smell, but by some other and subtler sense. He heard nothing, saw nothing, yet knew that the land was somehow different; that through it strange things were afoot and ranging; and he resolved to investigate after he had finished the business in hand.

At last, at the end of the fourth day, he pulled the great moose down. For a day and a night he remained by the kill, eating and sleeping, turn and turn about. Then, rested, refreshed and strong, he turned his face toward camp and John Thornton. He broke into the long easy lope, and went on, hour after hour, never at loss for the tangled way, heading straight for home through strange country with a certitude of direction that put man and his magnetic needle to shame.

As he held on he became more and more conscious of the new stir in the land. There was life abroad in it different from the life which had been there throughout the summer. No longer was this fact borne in upon him in some subtle, mysterious way. The birds talked of it, the squirrels chattered about it, the very breeze whispered of it. Several times he stopped and drew in the fresh morning air in great sniffs, reading a message which made him leap on with greater speed. He was oppressed with a sense of calamity happening, if it were not calamity already happened; and as he crossed the last watershed and dropped down into the valley toward camp, he proceeded with greater caution.

Three miles away he came upon a fresh trail that sent his neck hair rippling and bristling. It led straight toward camp and John Thornton. Buck hurried on, swiftly and stealthily, every nerve straining and tense, alert to the multitudinous details which told a story—all but the end. His nose gave him a varying description of the passage of the life on the heels of which he was traveling. He remarked the pregnant silence of the forest. The bird life had flitted. The squirrels were in hiding. One only he saw—a sleek gray fellow, flattened against a gray dead limb so that he seemed a part of it, a woody excrescence upon the wood itself.

As Buck slid along with the obscureness of a gliding shadow, his nose was jerked suddenly to the side as though a positive force had gripped and pulled it. He followed the new scent into a thicket and found Nig. He was lying on his side, dead where he had dragged himself, an arrow protruding, head and feathers, from either side of his body.

A hundred yards farther on, Buck came upon one of the sled-dogs Thornton had bought in Dawson. This dog was thrashing about in a death-struggle, directly on the trail, and Buck passed around him without stopping. From the camp came the faint sound of many voices, rising and falling in a sing-song chant. Bellying forward to the edge of the clearing, he found Hans, lying on his face, feathered with arrows like a porcupine. At the same instant Buck peered out where the spruce-bough lodge had been and saw what made his hair leap straight up on his neck and shoulders. A gust of overpowering rage swept over him. He did not know that he growled, but he growled aloud with a terrible ferocity. For the last time in his life he allowed passion to usurp cunning and reason, and it was because of his great love for John Thornton that he lost his head.

The Yeehats were dancing about the wreckage of the spruce-bough lodge when they heard a fearful roaring and saw rushing upon them an animal the like of which they had never seen before. It was Buck, a live hurricane of fury, hurling himself upon them in a frenzy to destroy. He sprang at the foremost man (it was the chief of the Yeehats), ripping the throat wide open till the rent jugular spouted a fountain of blood. He did not pause to worry the victim, but ripped in passing, with the next bound tearing wide the throat of a second man. There was no withstanding him. He plunged about in their inner midst, tearing, rending, destroying, in a constant and terrific motion which defied the arrows they discharged at him. In fact, so inconceivably rapid were his movements, and so closely were the Indians tangled together, that they shot one another with the arrows; and one young hunter, hurling a spear at Buck in mid air, drove it through the chest of another hunter with such force that the point broke through the skin of the back and stood out far beyond. Then a panic seized the Yeehats, and they fled in terror to the woods, proclaiming in flight the advent of the Evil Spirit.

And truly Buck was the Fiend incarnate raging at their heels and dragging them down like deer as they raced through the trees. It was a fateful day for the Yeehats. They scattered far and wide over the country, and it was not till a week later that the last of the survivors gathered together in a lower valley and counted their losses. As for Buck, wearying of the pursuit, he returned to the desolated camp. He found Pete where he had been killed in his blankets in the first moment of surprise. Thornton's desperate struggle was fresh-written on the earth, and Buck scented every detail of it down to the edge of a deep pool. By the edge, head and

"And beyond the fire, in darkness, Buck saw gleaming eyes."

10

forefeet in the water, lay Skeet, faithful to the last. The pool itself, muddy and discolored from the sluice boxes, effectually hid what it contained, and it contained John Thornton; for Buck followed his trace into the water, from which no trace led away.

All day Buck brooded by the pool or roamed restlessly about the camp. Death, as a cessation of movement, as a passing out and away from the lives of the living, he knew, and he knew John Thornton was dead. It left a great void in him, somewhat akin to hunger, but a void which ached and ached, and which food could not fill. At times, when he paused to contemplate the carcasses of the Yeehats, he forgot the pain of it; and at such times he was aware of a great pride in himself—a pride greater than any

the open space and listened. It was the call, the many-noted call, sounding more luringly and compelling than ever before. And as never before, he was ready to obey. John Thornton was dead. The last tie was broken. Man and the claims of man no longer bound him.

Hunting their living meat, as the Yeehats were hunting it, on the flanks of the migrating moose, the wolf pack had at last crossed over from the land of streams and timber and invaded Buck's valley. Into the clearing where the moonlight streamed, they poured in a silvery flood; and in the center of the clearing stood Buck, motionless as a statue, waiting their coming. They were awed, so still and large he stood, and a moment's pause fell, till the

"Buck led the pack as, leap by leap, like some pale frost wraith, the snowshoe rabbit flashed on ahead."

he had yet experienced. He had killed man, the noblest game of all, and he had killed in the face of the law of club and fang. He sniffed the bodies curiously. They had died so easily. It was harder to kill a husky dog than them. They were no match at all, were it not for their arrows and spears and clubs. Thenceforward he would be unafraid of them except when they bore in their hands their arrows, spears and clubs.

Night came on, and a full moon rose high over the trees into the sky, lighting the land till it lay bathed in ghostly day. And with the coming of the night, brooding and mourning by the pool, Buck became alive to a stirring of the new life in the forest other than that which the Yeehats had made. He stood up, listening and scenting. From far away drifted a faint, sharp yelp, followed by a chorus of similar sharp yelps. As the moments passed the yelps grew closer and louder. Again Buck knew them as things heard in that other world which persisted in his memory. He walked to the center of

boldest one leaped straight for him. Like a flash Buck struck, breaking the neck. Then he stood, as before, the stricken wolf rolling in agony behind him. Three others tried it in sharp succession; and one after the other they drew back, streaming blood from slashed throats or shoulders.

This was sufficient to fling the whole pack forward, pell-mell, crowded together, blocked and confused by its eagerness to pull down the prey. Buck's marvelous quickness and agility stood him in good stead. Pivoting on his hind legs, and snapping and gashing, he was everywhere at once, presenting a front which was apparently unbroken so swiftly did he whirl and guard from side to side. But to prevent them from getting behind him, he was forced back, down past the pool and into the creek bed, till he brought up against a high gravel bank. He worked along to a right angle in the bank which the men had made in the course of mining, and in this angle he came to bay, protected on three sides and with nothing to do but face the front.

And so well did he face it that at the end of half an hour the wolves drew back discomfited. The tongues of all were out and lolling, the white fangs showing cruelly white in the moonlight. Some were lying down with heads raised and ears pricked forward; others stood on their feet, watching him; and still others were lapping water from the pool. One wolf, long and lean and gray, advanced cautiously, in a friendly manner, and Buck recognized the wild brother with whom he had run for a night and a day. He was whining softly, and, as Buck whined, they touched noses.

Then an old wolf, battle-scarred and gaunt, stepped forward. Buck writhed his lips into the preliminary of a snarl, but sniffed noses with him. Whereupon the old wolf sat down, pointed nose at the moon, and broke out the long wolf howl. The others sat down and howled. And now the call came to Buck in unmistakable accents. He, too, sat down and howled. This over, he came out of his angle and the pack crowded all around him, sniffing in half-friendly, half-savage manner. The leaders lifted the yelp of the pack and sprang away into the woods. The wolves swung in behind, yelping in chorus. And Buck ran with them, side by side with the wild brother.

And here may well end the story of Buck. The years were not many when the Yeehats noted a change in the breed of timber wolves; for some were seen with splashes of brown on head and muzzle, and with a rift of white centering down the chest. But more remarkable than this, the Yeehats tell of a Ghost Dog that runs at the head of the

"Under the shimmering borealis he sings the song of a younger world."

pack. They are afraid of this Ghost Dog, for it has cunning greater than they, stealing from their camps in fierce winters, robbing their traps, slaying their dogs, and defying the bravest hunters.

Nay, the tale grows worse. Hunters there are who fail to return to the camp, and hunters there have been whom their tribesmen found with throats slashed cruelly open and with wolf prints about them in the snow greater than the prints of any wolf. Each fall, when the Yeehats follow the movement of the moose, there is a particular valley which they dare not enter. And women there are who become sad when the word goes over the fire of how the Evil Spirit came to select that valley for an abiding-place.

In the summers there is one visitor, however, to that valley, of which the Yeehats do not know. It is a great, magnificently coated wolf, like, and yet unlike, all the other wolves. He crosses alone from the smiling timber land and comes down into an open space among the trees. Here a yellow stream flows from rotted moose-hide sacks and sinks into the ground, with long grasses growing through it and vegetable mould overrunning it and hiding its yellow from the sun; and here he muses for a time, howling once, long and mournfully, ere he departs.

But he is not always alone. When the long winter nights come on and the wolves follow their meat into the lower valleys, he may be seen running at the head of the pack through the pale moonlight or glimmering borealis, leaping gigantic above his fellows, his great throat a-bellow as he sings a song of the younger world, which is the song of the pack.

THE BEAR
by William Faulkner

He was ten. But it had already begun, long before that day when at last he wrote his age in two figures and he saw for the first time the camp where his father and Major de Spain and old General Compson and the others spent two weeks each November and two weeks again each June. He had already inherited then, without ever having seen it, the tremendous bear with one trap-ruined foot which, in an area almost a hundred miles deep, had earned for itself a name, a definite designation like a living man.

He had listened to it for years: the long legend of corncribs rifled, of shoats and grown pigs and even calves carried bodily into the woods and devoured, of traps and deadfalls overthrown and dogs mangled and slain, and shotgun and even rifle charges delivered at point-blank range and with no more effect than so many peas blown through a tube by a boy—a corridor of wreckage and destruction beginning back before he was born, through which sped, not fast but rather with the ruthless and irresistible deliberation of a locomotive, the shaggy tremendous shape.

It ran in his knowledge before he ever saw it. It looked and towered in his dreams before he even saw the unaxed woods where it left its crooked print, shaggy, huge, red-eyed, not malevolent but just big—too big for the dogs which tried to bay it, for the horses which tried to ride it down, for the men and the bullets they fired into it, too big for the very country which was its constricting scope. He seemed to see it entire with a child's complete divination before he ever laid eyes on either—the doomed wilderness whose edges were being constantly and punily gnawed at by men with axes and plows who feared it because it was wilderness, men myriad and nameless even to one another in the land where the old bear had earned a name, through which ran not even a mortal animal but an anachronism, indomitable and invincible, out of an

This story was first published in the Post *in 1942. Boy and bear reappeared in Faulkner's novel* Go Down, Moses.

old dead time, a phantom, epitome and apotheosis of the old wild life at which the puny humans swarmed and hacked in a fury of abhorrence and fear, like pygmies about the ankles of a drowsing elephant; the old bear solitary, indomitable and alone, widowered, childless and absolved of mortality—old Priam reft of his old wife and having outlived all of his sons.

Until he was ten, each November he would watch the wagon containing the dogs and the bedding and food and guns and his father and Tennie's Jim, the Negro, and Sam Fathers, the Indian, son of a slave woman and a Chickasaw chief, depart on the road to town, to Jefferson, where Major de Spain and the others would join them. To the boy, at seven and eight and nine, they were not going into the Big Bottom to hunt bear and deer, but to keep yearly rendezvous with the bear which they did not even intend to kill. Two weeks later they would return, with no trophy, no head and skin. He had not expected it. He had not even been afraid it would be in the wagon. He believed that even after he was ten and his father would let him go too, for those two November weeks, he would merely make another one, along with his father and Major de Spain and General Compson and the others, the dogs which feared to bay it and the rifles and shotguns which failed even to bleed it in the yearly pageant of the old bear's furious immortality.

Then he heard the dogs. It was in the second week of his first time in the camp. He stood with Sam Fathers against a big oak beside the faint crossing where they had stood each dawn for nine days now, hearing the dogs. He had heard them once before, one morning last week—a murmur, sourceless, echoing through the wet woods, swelling presently into separate voices which he could recognize and call by name. He had raised and cocked the gun as Sam told him and stood motionless again while the uproar, the invisible course, swept up and past and faded; it seemed to him that he could actually see the deer, the buck, blond, smoke-colored, elongated with speed, fleeing, vanishing, the woods, the gray solitude, still ringing even when the cries of the dogs had died away.

"Now let the hammers down," Sam said.

"You knew they were not coming here too," he said.

"Yes," Sam said. "I want you to learn how to do when you didn't shoot. It's after the chance for the bear or the deer has done already come and gone that men and dogs get killed."

"Anyway," he said, "it was just a deer."

Then on the tenth morning he heard the dogs again. And he readied the too-long, too-heavy gun as Sam had taught him, before Sam even spoke. But this time it was no deer, no ringing chorus of dogs running strong on a free scent, but a moiling yapping an octave too high, with something more than indecision and even abjectness in it, not even moving very fast, taking a long time to pass completely out of hearing, leaving even then somewhere in the air that echo, thin, slightly hysterical, abject, almost grieving, with no sense of a fleeing, unseen, smoke-colored, grass-eating shape ahead of it, and Sam, who had taught him first of all to cock the gun and take position where he could see everywhere and then never move again, had himself moved up beside him; he could hear Sam breathing at his shoulder and he could see the arched curve of the old man's inhaling nostrils.

"Hah," Sam said. "Not even running. Walking."

"Old Ben!" the boy said. "But up here!" he cried. "Way up here!"

"He do it every year," Sam said. "Once. Maybe to see who in camp this time, if he can shoot or not. Whether we got the dog yet that can bay and hold him. He'll take them to the river, then he'll send them back home. We may as well go back, too; see how they look when they come back to camp."

When they reached the camp the hounds were already there, ten of them crouching back under the kitchen, the boy and Sam squatting to peer back into the obscurity where they huddled, quiet, the eyes luminous, glowing at them and vanishing, and no sound, only that effluvium of something more than dog, stronger than dog and not just animal, just beast, because still there had been nothing in front of that abject and almost painful yapping save the solitude, the wilderness, so that when the eleventh hound came in at noon and with all the others watching—even old Uncle Ash, who called himself first a cook—Sam daubed the tattered ear and the raked shoulder with turpentine and axle grease, to the boy it was still no living creature, but the wilderness which, leaning for the moment down, had patted lightly once the hound's temerity.

"Just like a man," Sam said. "Just like folks. Put off as long as she could having to be brave, knowing all the time that sooner or later she would have to be brave once to keep on living with herself, and knowing all the time beforehand just what was going to happen to her when she done it."

That afternoon, himself on the one-eyed wagon mule which did not mind the smell of blood nor, as they told him, of bear, and with Sam on the other one, they rode for more than three hours through the rapid, shortening winter day. They followed no path, no trail even that he could see; almost at once they were in a country which he had never seen before. Then he knew why Sam had made him ride the mule which would not spook. The sound one stopped short and tried to whirl and bolt even as Sam got down, blowing its breath, jerking and wrenching at the rein while Sam held it, coaxing it forward with his voice, since he could not risk tying it, drawing it forward while the boy got down from the marred one.

Then, standing beside Sam in the gloom of the dying afternoon, he looked down at the rotted overturned log, gutted and scored with claw marks and, in the wet earth beside it, the print of the enormous warped two-toed foot. He knew now what he had smelled when he peered under the kitchen where the dogs huddled. He realized for the first time that the bear which had run in his listening and loomed in his dreams since before he could

14

remember to the contrary, and which, therefore, must have existed in the listening and dreams of his father and Major de Spain and even old General Compson, too, was a mortal animal, and that if they had departed for the camp each November without any actual hope of bringing its trophy back, it was not because it could not be slain, but because so far they had had no actual hope to.

"Tomorrow," he said.

"We'll try tomorrow," Sam said. "We ain't got the dog yet."

"We've got eleven. They ran him this morning."

"It won't need but one," Sam said. "He ain't here. Maybe he ain't nowhere. The only other way will be for him to run by accident over somebody that has a gun."

"That wouldn't boy said. "It will be Major or——"

"It might," Sam watch close in the cause he's smart. come he has If he gets and has to pick to run over, he you."

"How?"

"How will he ceased. "You knows me— been here time to whether again the old face until it

be me," the Walter or

said. "You morning. Be- That's how lived this long. hemmed up out somebody will pick out

the boy said. know——"He mean he already that I ain't never before, ain't had find out yet I——" He ceased looking at Sam, man whose lined revealed nothing smiled. He said humbly, not even

Bears once roamed the entire northern hemisphere; Alaska's brown bears were the largest.

CHARLES LIVINGSTON BULL.

amazed, "It was me he was watching. I don't reckon he did need to come but once."

The next morning they left the camp three hours before daylight. They rode this time because it was too far to walk, even the dogs in the wagon; again the first gray light found him in a place which he had never seen before, where Sam had placed him and told him to stay and then departed. With the gun which was too big for him, which did not even belong to him, but to Major de Spain, and which he had fired only once—at a stump on the first day, to learn the recoil and how to reload it—he stood against a gum tree beside a little bayou whose black still water crept without movement out of a canebrake and crossed a small clearing and into cane again, where, invisible, a bird—the big woodpecker called Lord-to-God by Negroes—clattered at a dead limb.

It was a stand like any other, dissimilar only in incidentals to the one where he had stood each morning for ten days; a territory new to him, yet no less familiar than that other one which, after almost two weeks, he had come to believe he knew a little—the same solitude, the same loneliness through which human beings had merely passed without altering it, leaving no mark, no scar, which looked exactly as it must have looked when the first ancestor of Sam Fathers' Chickasaw predecessors crept into it and looked about, club or stone ax or bone arrow drawn and poised; different only because, squatting at the

"They had met for two weeks to fish and shoot squirrels and run coons. . . . "

edge of the kitchen, he smelled the hounds huddled and cringing beneath it and saw the raked ear and shoulder of the one who, Sam said, had had to be brave once in order to live with herself, and saw yesterday in the earth beside the gutted log the prints of the living foot.

He heard no dogs at all. He never did hear them. He only heard the drumming of the woodpecker stop short off and knew that the bear was looking at him. He never saw it. He did not know whether it was in front of him or behind him. He did not

move, holding the useless gun, which he had not even had warning to cock and which even now he did not cock, tasting in his saliva that taint as of brass which he knew now because he had smelled it when he peered under the kitchen at the huddled dogs.

Then it was gone. As abruptly as it had ceased, the woodpecker's dry, monotonous clatter set up again, and after a while he even believed he could hear the dogs—a murmur, scarce a sound even, which he had probably been hearing for some time before he even remarked it, drifting into hearing and then out again, dying away. They came nowhere near him. If it was a bear they ran, it was another bear. It was Sam himself who came out of the cane and crossed the bayou, followed by the injured bitch of yesterday. She was almost at heel, like a bird dog, making no sound. She came and crouched against his leg, trembling, staring off into the cane.

"I didn't see him," he said. "I didn't, Sam!"

"I know it," Sam said. "He done the looking. You didn't hear him neither, did you?"

"No," the boy said. "I——"

"He's smart," Sam said. "Too smart." He looked down at the hound, trembling faintly and steadily against the boy's knee. From the raked shoulder a few drops of fresh blood oozed and clung. "Too big. We ain't got the dog yet. But maybe someday. Maybe not next time. But someday."

So I must see him, he thought. *I must look at him.* Otherwise, it seemed to him that it would go on like this forever, as it had gone on with his father and Major de Spain, who was older than his father, and even with old General Compson, who had been old enough to be a brigade commander in 1865. Otherwise, it would go on so forever, next time and next time, after and after and after. It seemed to him that he could see the two of them, himself and the bear, shadowy in the limbo from which time emerged, becoming time; the old bear absolved of

16

mortality and himself partaking, sharing a little of it, enough of it. And he knew now what he had smelled in the huddled dogs and tasted in his saliva. He recognized fear. *So I will have to see him,* he thought, without dread or even hope. *I will have to look at him.*

It was in June of the next year. He was eleven. They were in camp again, celebrating Major de Spain's and General Compson's birthdays. Although the one had been born in September and the other in the depth of winter and in another decade, they had met for two weeks to fish and shoot squirrels and turkey and run coons and wildcats with the dogs at night. That is, he and Boon Hoggenbeck and the Negroes fished and shot squirrels and ran the coons and cats, because the proved hunters, not only Major de Spain and old General Compson, who spent those two weeks sitting in a rocking chair before a tremendous iron pot of Brunswick stew, stirring and tasting, with old Ash to quarrel with about how he was making it and Tennie's Jim to pour whisky from the demijohn into the tin dipper from which he drank it, but even the boy's father and Walter Ewell, who were still young enough, scorned such, other than shooting the wild gobblers with pistols for wagers on their marksmanship.

"Each morning he would leave the camp after breakfast. He had his own gun now, a Christmas present."

Or, that is, his father and the others believed he was hunting squirrels. Until the third day he thought that Sam Fathers believed that too. Each morning he would leave the camp right after breakfast. He had his own gun now, a Christmas present. He went back to the tree beside the little bayou where he had stood that morning. Using the compass which old General Compson had given him, he ranged from that point; he was teaching himself to be a better-than-fair woodsman without knowing he was doing it. On the second day he even found the gutted log where he had first seen the crooked print. It was almost completely crumbled now, healing with unbelievable speed, a passionate and almost visible relinquishment, back into the earth from which the trees of the forest had grown.

He ranged the summer woods now, green with gloom; if anything, actually dimmer than in November's gray dissolution, where, even at noon, the sun fell only in intermittent dappling upon the earth, which never completely dried out and which crawled with snakes—moccasins and water snakes and rattlers, themselves the color of the dappled gloom, so that he would not always see them until they moved, returning later and later, first day, second day, passing in the twilight of the third evening the little log pen enclosing the log stable where Sam was putting up the horses for the night.

"You ain't looked right yet," Sam said.

He stopped. For a moment he didn't answer. Then he said peacefully, in a peaceful rushing burst as when a boy's miniature dam in a little brook gives way, "All right. But how? I went to the bayou. I even found that log again. I——"

"I reckon that was all right. Likely he's been watching you. You never saw his bad foot?"

"I," the boy said—"I didn't see it—I never thought——"

"It's the gun," Sam said. He stood beside the fence, motionless—the old man, the Indian, in the battered faded overalls and the frayed five-cent straw hat which in the Negro's race had been the badge of his enslavement and was now the regalia of his freedom. The camp—the clearing, the house, the barn and its tiny lot with which Major de Spain in his turn had scratched punily and evanescently at the wilderness—faded in the dusk, back into the immemorial darkness of the woods. *The gun,* the boy thought. *The gun.*

"Be scared," Sam said. "You can't help that. But don't be afraid. Ain't nothing in the woods going to hurt you unless you corner it, or it smells that you are afraid. A bear or a deer, too, has got to be scared of a coward the same as a brave man has got to be."

The gun, the boy thought.

"You will have to choose," Sam said.

He left the camp before daylight, long before Uncle Ash would wake in his quilts on the kitchen

17

"The secret night sounds scurried again and ceased, and the owls ceased and gave over to the waking of day birds."

floor and start the fire for breakfast. He had only the compass and a stick for snakes. He could go almost a mile before he would begin to need the compass. He sat on a log, the invisible compass in his invisible hand, while the secret night sounds, fallen still at his movements, scurried again and then ceased for good, and the owls ceased and gave over to the waking of day birds, and he could see the compass. Then he went fast yet still quietly; he was becoming better and better as a woodsman, still without having yet realized it.

He jumped a doe and a fawn at sunrise, walked them out of the bed, close enough to see them—the crash of undergrowth, the white scut, the fawn scudding behind her faster than he had believed it could run. He was hunting right, upwind, as Sam

had taught him; not that it mattered now. He had left the gun; of his own will and relinquishment he had accepted not a gambit, not a choice, but a condition in which not only the bear's heretofore inviolable anonymity but all the old rules and balances of hunter and hunted had been abrogated. He would not even be afraid, not even in the moment when the fear would take him completely—blood, skin, bowels, bones, memory from the long time before it became his memory—all save that thin, clear, quenchless, immortal lucidity which alone differed him from this bear and from all the other bear and deer he would ever kill in the humility and pride of his skill and endurance, to which Sam had spoken when he leaned in the twilight on the lot fence yesterday.

18

By noon he was far beyond the little bayou, farther into the new and alien country than he had ever been. He was traveling now not only by the compass but by the old, heavy, biscuit-thick silver watch which had belonged to his grandfather. When he stopped at last, it was for the first time since he had risen from the log at dawn when he could see the compass. It was far enough. He had left the camp nine hours ago; nine hours from now, dark would have already been an hour old. But he didn't think that. He thought, *All right. Yes. But what?* and stood for a moment, alien and small in the green and topless solitude, answering his own question before it had formed and ceased. It was the watch, the compass, the—the three lifeless mechanicals with which for nine hours he had fended the wilderness off; he hung the watch and compass carefully on a bush and leaned the stick beside them and relinquished completely to it.

He had not been going very fast for the last two or three hours. He went no faster now, since distance would not matter even if he could have gone fast. And he was trying to keep a bearing on the tree where he had left the compass, trying to complete a circle which would bring him back to it or at least intersect itself, since direction would not matter now either. But the tree was not there, and he did as Sam had schooled him—made the next circle in the opposite direction, so that the two patterns would bisect somewhere, but crossing no print of his own feet, finding the tree at last, but in the wrong place—no bush, no compass, no watch—and the tree not even the tree, because there was a down log beside it and he did what Sam Fathers had told him was the next thing and the last.

As he sat down on the log he saw the crooked print—the warped, tremendous, two-toed indentation which, even as he watched it, filled with water. As he looked up, the wilderness coalesced, solidified—the glade, the tree he sought, the bush, the watch and the compass glinting where a ray of sunlight touched them.

Then he saw the bear. It did not emerge, appear; it was just there, immobile, solid, fixed in the hot dappling of the green and windless noon, not as big as he had dreamed it, but as big as he had expected it, bigger, dimensionless against the dappled obscurity, looking at him where he sat quietly on the log and looked back at it.

Then it moved. It made no

"He was . . . further into the new and alien country than he had ever been."

19

sound. It did not hurry. It crossed the glade, walking for an instant into the full glare of the sun; when it reached the other side it stopped again and looked back at him across one shoulder while his quiet breathing inhaled and exhaled three times.

Then it was gone. It didn't walk into the woods, the undergrowth. It faded, sank back into the wilderness as he had watched a fish, a huge old bass, sink and vanish back into the dark depths of its pool without even any movement of its fins.

He thought, *It will be next fall.* But it was not next fall, nor the next nor the next. He was fourteen then. He had killed his buck, and Sam Fathers had marked his face with the hot blood, and in the next year he killed a bear. But even before that accolade he had become as competent in the woods as many grown men with the same experience; by his fourteenth year he was a better woodsman than most grown men with more. There was no territory within thirty miles of the camp that he did not know—bayou, ridge, brake, landmark tree and path. He could have led anyone to any point in it without deviation, and brought them out again. He knew game trails that even Sam Fathers did not know; in his thirteenth year he found a buck's bedding place, and unbeknown to his father he borrowed Walter Ewell's rifle and lay in wait at dawn and killed the buck when it walked back to the bed, as Sam had told him how the old Chickasaw fathers did.

After he had seen the old bear, he knew what Sam Fathers had meant about the right dog, a dog in which size would mean less than nothing. So when he returned alone in April—school was out then, so that the sons of farmers could help with the land's planting, and at last his father had granted him permission, on his promise to be back in four days—he had the dog. It was his own, a mongrel of the sort called by Negroes a fyce, a ratter, itself not much bigger than a rat and possessing that bravery which had long since stopped being courage and had become foolhardiness.

It did not take four days. Alone again, he found the trail on the first morning. It was not a stalk; it was an ambush. He timed the meeting almost as if it were an appointment with a human being. Himself holding the fyce muffled in a feed sack and Sam Fathers with two of the hounds on a piece of plowline rope, they lay downwind of the trail at dawn of the second morning. They were so close that the bear turned without even running, as if in surprised amazement at the shrill and frantic uproar of the released fyce, turning at bay against the trunk of a tree, on its hind feet; it seemed to the boy that it would never stop rising, taller and taller, and even the two hounds seemed to take a sort of desperate and despairing courage from the fyce, following it as it went in.

Then he realized that the fyce was actually not going to stop. He flung, threw the gun away, and ran; when he overtook and grasped the frantically pinwheeling little dog, it seemed to him that he was directly under the bear.

He could smell it, strong and hot and rank. Sprawling, he looked up to where it loomed and towered over him like a cloudburst and colored like a thunderclap, quite familiar, peacefully and even lucidly familiar, until he remembered: This was the way he had used to dream about it. Then it was gone. He didn't see it go. He knelt, holding the frantic fyce with both hands, hearing the abased wailing of the hounds drawing farther and farther away, until Sam came up. He carried the gun. He laid it down quietly beside the boy and stood looking down at him.

"You've done seed him twice now with a gun in your hands," he said. "This time you couldn't have missed him."

The boy rose. He still held the fyce. Even in his arms and clear of the ground, it yapped frantically, straining and surging after the fading uproar of the two hounds like a tangle of wire springs. He was panting a little, but he was neither shaking nor trembling now.

"Neither could you!" he said. "You had the gun! Neither did you!"

"He was becoming better and better as a woodsman, still without realizing it. He jumped a doe and a fawn at sunrise."

"And you didn't shoot," his father said. "How close were you?"

"I don't know, sir," he said. "There was a big wood tick inside his right hind leg. I saw that. But I didn't have the gun then."

"But you didn't shoot when you had the gun," his father said.

"Why?" But he didn't answer, and his father didn't wait for him to, rising and crossing the room, across the pelt of the bear which the boy had killed two years ago and the larger one which his father had killed before he was born, to the bookcase beneath the mounted head of the boy's first buck. It was the room which his father called the office, from which all the plantation business was transacted; in it for the fourteen years of his life he had heard the best of all talking. Major de Spain would be there and sometimes old General Compson, and Walter Ewell and Boon Hoggenbeck and Sam Fathers and Tennie's Jim, too, because they, too, were hunters, knew the woods and what ran them.

He would hear it, not talking himself but listening—the wilderness, the big woods, bigger and older than any recorded document of white man fatuous enough to believe he had bought any fragment of it or Indian ruthless enough to pretend that any fragment of it had been his to convey. It was of the men, not white nor black nor red, but men, hunters with the will and hardihood to endure and the humility and skill to survive, and the dogs and the bear and deer juxtaposed and reliefed against it, ordered and compelled by and within the wilderness in the ancient and unremitting contest by the ancient and immitigable rules which voided all regrets and brooked no quarter, the voices quiet and weighty and deliberate for retrospection and recollection and exact remembering, while he squatted in the blazing firelight as Tennie's Jim squatted,

21

who stirred only to put more wood on the fire and to pass the bottle from one glass to another. Because the bottle was always present, so that after a while it seemed to him that those fierce instants of heart and brain and courage and wiliness and speed were concentrated and distilled into that brown liquor which not women, not boys and children, but only hunters drank, drinking not of the blood they had spilled but some condensation of the wild immortal spirit, drinking it moderately, humbly even, not with the pagan's base hope of acquiring thereby the virtues of cunning and strength and speed, but in salute to them.

His father returned with the book and sat down again and opened it. "Listen," he said. He read the second stanza to the end and closed the book and put it on the table beside him. " 'She cannot fade, though thou hast not thy bliss, for ever wilt thou love, and she be fair,' " he said.

"He's talking about a girl," the boy said.

"He had to talk about something," his father said. Then he said, "He was talking about truth. Truth doesn't change. Truth is one thing. It covers all things which touch the heart—honor and pride and pity and justice and courage and love. Do you see now?"

He didn't know. Somehow it was simpler than that. There was an old bear, fierce and ruthless, not merely just to stay alive, but with the fierce pride of liberty and freedom, proud enough of that liberty and freedom to see it threatened without fear or even alarm; nay, who at times even seemed deliberately to put that freedom and liberty in jeopardy in order to savor them, to remind his old strong bones and flesh to keep supple and quick to defend and preserve them. There was an old man, son of a

"There was an old bear, fierce and ruthless, not merely to stay alive, but with the fierce pride of liberty and freedom, proud enough of that liberty and freedom to see it threatened without fear."

Negro slave and an Indian king, inheritor on the one side of the long chronicle of a people who had learned humility through suffering, and pride through the endurance which survived the suffering and injustice, and on the other side, the chronicle of a people even longer in the land than the first, yet who no longer existed in the land at all save in the solitary brotherhood of an old Negro's alien blood and the wild and invincible spirit of an old bear. There was a boy who wished to learn humility and pride in order to become skillful and worthy in the woods, who suddenly found himself becoming so skillful so rapidly that he feared he would not ever become worthy because he had not learned humility and pride, although he had tried to, until one day and as suddenly he discovered that an old man who could not have defined either had led him, as though by the hand, to that point where an old bear and a little mongrel dog showed him that, by possessing one thing other, he would possess them both.

And a little dog, nameless and mongrel and many-fathered, grown, yet weighing less than six pounds, saying as if to itself, "I can't be dangerous, because there's nothing much smaller than I am; I can't be fierce, because they would call it just noise; I can't be humble, because I'm already too close to the ground to genuflect; I can't be proud, because I wouldn't be near enough to it for anyone to know who was casting that shadow, and I don't even know that I'm not going to heaven, because they have already decided that I don't possess an immortal soul. So all I can be is brave. But it's all right. I can be that, even if they still call it just noise."

That was all.

LANDSCAPE WITH ANIMALS

COLUMBUS SAW IT FIRST

by Roger Tory Peterson

Columbus may have been our first bird-watcher. After he left the Canary Islands, birds became the most important entries in his log. As he sailed west into the unknown, his men grew sullen and threatening. At this critical time flocks of birds "coming from the N and making for the SW" gave them heart. Columbus turned his course in the direction the birds were flying and in due time reached the Bahamas. Had he not followed the birds or had he left the Canaries two weeks later, after the heavy fall migration was past, his first landfall might have been the coast of

Florida—if indeed there had been a landfall. His men were close to mutiny and the extra two hundred miles might have been the difference between success and failure.

Every ornithologist I know would give his soul to step back into time and walk the continent in the historic year of 1492. It was all virgin country then, with trees centuries old and the native grass waist high on the prairies. The broad distributional concepts—the life zones or the biomes—probably would have been much more satisfactory in those days when most environments were in relatively stable "climaxes," as the old mature plant associations are called. But that was before man set in motion the constant chain of changes that take place wherever he goes. For civilized man is the great disturber. Some would call him a destroyer, but that I think is a harsh term. Certainly he brings change.

There is a vague idea that birds were far more abundant in primeval America than they are now. In 1614, six years before the Pilgrims landed at Plymouth, John Smith sailed down the coast of Maine. He wrote of the incredible abundance of wildlife which he observed: "eagles, gripes, divers sort of hauks, cranes, geese, brants, cormorants, ducks, sheldrakes, teals, meawes, guls, turkies, divedoppers, and many other sorts, whose names I knowe not."

In the early days there were no game laws, but it did not take long to realize that there would have to be some kind of brake on the killing. The first legal regulations were imposed in New Netherlands more than 300 years ago. At the close of the colonial period, twelve of the thirteen colonies had some sort of game laws. Since then restrictions have grown tighter and tighter, for an army of millions of American men now go out with guns each year, fully as many as were pressed into service to fight the greatest war the world has ever known. One to two millions purchase the Duck Stamp. The wildfowlers have grown legion, even though there are alive today only a fraction of the ducks that swarmed the flyways when John Smith cruised the coast.

The ducks may be down, but some of the other birds are well up and still climbing. Let us look briefly at the score sheet and see which way our birds are going.

Most of the waterfowl and the native upland game birds are below par. There has been some restoration in places, but there were many more of them in primitive America. Even twentieth-century America could support more than it does. Hunting often exacts a greater toll than the traffic will bear.

Today all marsh birds, not waterfowl alone, are in the red. Every day plans are made somewhere in this country to drain a lake, a swamp or a marsh. The records show that close to 100 million acres of land have been drained in the United States for agriculture alone. Other millions of acres have been ditched to control mosquitoes. Considering that a marsh or swamp habitat harbors nine or ten nesting birds per acre and most farming country an average of fewer than three, this means that at least half a billion birds may have been eliminated from the face of the continent by the simple process of digging ditches.

The birds of prey—the hawks and the owls—are much reduced. One summer day in 1947, John Craighead, the well-known falconer, and I paddled

In his journal for October 7, 1492, Columbus reported "a great multitude of birds" overhead. He happened to be in the direct line of flight for birds migrating from North America to the West Indies via Bermuda at that time of year.

a rubber boat down the Snake River in Wyoming. There in the dome of the sky that vaulted the  magnificent Teton Valley, the hawks were never out of sight—circling red-tails and Swainson's hawks, swift-flying prairie falcons, even eagles. It gave me an inkling of what the normal conditions must have been in aboriginal America. Yet the gunner often blamed the growing scarcity of game not on himself but on the natural predators, which had lived in satisfactory adjustment to their prey for thousands of years. He called all hawks "vermin," competitors to be shot and destroyed. And the skies over most of America today are still not empty enough of hawks to satisfy him.

The vultures, on the other hand, seem to be spreading. The turkey vulture, pushing northward in the Appalachians, followed the return of the deer to the Hudson highlands, and can now be found in the Berkshires in Connecticut. Its intelligent, aggressive cousin, the black vulture, has bypassed Washington, D.C., and is invading Maryland.

The gulls and terns were shot and egged almost out of existence by 1900, but in less than fifty years they have made a complete comeback. Most species seem to be as numerous as they ever were. The shore birds, too—"snipe" in the gunners' language—nearly faded from the beaches; but since they have been excluded from the game bags, many of them have returned. The herons are also doing very well. The two white egrets almost crossed the Styx; the pirates of the millinery trade nearly got them all. With protection, these immaculate waders have skyrocketed from a few hundred, perhaps a few thousand, to hundreds of thousands.

And what about the songbirds? In earlier days they were caged; they went into potpies; and boys made collections of their eggs. People no longer do these things. It is easier for most of us to get sentimental about a chickadee or a song sparrow than a duck or a grouse. Inconsistent though it may be, the smaller a thing is the more we want to protect it. I remember the winter day a young ornithologist shot a pine grosbeak. He had very good reason for doing so, but when he showed his scientific collecting permit to the game protector who intercepted him, the warden's only comment was "I still think it's a damned shame." Yet this same warden killed hawks, even the protected ones, like the red-shouldered, and he always liked to get in a few days of grouse shooting each fall.

Although songbirds are no longer persecuted, a few species have declined because their environment has changed; but for every one of these there must be a half dozen that are more common today than they ever were. The reason for this is logical. Wherever man goes, down comes the wilderness. The ringing ax starts plant succession all over again. The majority of songbirds find their niche in the development stages of plant growth; relatively few are obligated to the mature timber.

Audubon found the chestnut-sided warbler only once in all the years he roamed America. "In the beginning of May, 1808," he wrote, "I shot five of these birds on a very cold morning near Pottsgrove, in the State of Pennsylvania. I have never met with a single individual of this species since. Where this species goes to breed I am unable to say. I can only suppose it must be far to the northward, as I ransacked the borders of Lake Ontario and those of Lakes Erie and Michigan without meeting with it. I do not know of any naturalist who has been more fortunate; otherwise I should here quote his observations."

At that time the big timber still covered most of the Northeast. Today the chestnut-side is a common bird. In New England its bright song rings from every brushy slope and clearing. On John Baker's 700-acre farm in Dutchess County, New York, this little sprite with the yellow cap and rufous sides is the most numerous bird at this stage of plant succession, when abandoned pastures are being reclaimed by low scrub. In recent years it has spread down the Appalachian plateau; it has become common in Audubon's Pennsylvania, and, following the scrubby thickets under the blighted chestnuts up in the mountains, the bird has made a spectacular appearance as far south as Georgia. In primeval America, when the trees were big, birds like the chestnut-side must have depended almost entirely on windfalls and lightning-ignited forest fires. These Acts of God were their only chance of survival. In a lumbered America there is much more room for them. But there are all sorts of

The mockingbird is common in areas where it was unknown a few decades ago, making itself at home in suburban gardens, city parks.

lumbering practices. Selective cropping of the timber is better for wildlife than the wasteful policy of "cut out and get out."

I am willing to wager there are many more indigo buntings today than there were in Audubon's time. As we drive across the Appalachian hills in July we hear, through the open windows of the car, more of these bright blue finches than of any other bird. True, there were probably more woodpeckers and more vireos in Audubon's day than there are now, but we have far more indigo buntings, song sparrows, robins, catbirds, thrashers, orioles, cardinals, mockingbirds, redstarts, phoebes, kingbirds, waxwings, prairie warblers, chats, goldfinches, towhees and field sparrows.

In brief, the larger birds are down; the smaller birds are doing well. Gunning, when it has not been wisely regulated, and marsh drainage have been the two most damaging factors that civilization has imposed on the birds, except for recent pesticides. On the other hand, we believe man's disturbance of the land, for better or worse, has made most of the countryside more suitable for songbirds. But we don't know for sure. Perhaps the virgin forests, by their very diversity, had much higher populations than the uniform second-growth woodlands of today. To offset this, civilization has created enormous amounts of "edge," has scrambled the plant communities, and has kept the green growth in such a constant state of succession that there well may be far more songbirds on the continent now than in the days of the Pilgrim fathers— perhaps more by a billion or two.

We can only guess.

(1948)

The great blue heron's numbers dwindle as marshes are dredged, drained, turned into farm fields or housing sites.

THE BEAUTIFUL OHIO
by John James Audubon

than ever landscape painter portrayed, or poet imagined.

The days were yet warm. The sun had assumed the rich and glowing hue which at that season produces the singular phenomenon called there the "Indian Summer." The moon had rather passed the meridian of her grandeur. We glided down the river, meeting no other ripple of the water than that formed by the propulsion of our boat. Leisurely we moved, gazing all day on the grandeur and beauty of the wild scenery around us.

Now and then a large catfish rose to the surface of the water, in pursuit of a shoal of fry, which, starting simultaneously from the liquid element like so many silver arrows, produced a shower of light, while the pursuer with open jaws seized the stragglers, and, with a splash of his tail, disappeared from our view. Other fishes we heard, uttering beneath our bark a rumbling noise, the strange sound of which we discovered to proceed from the white perch, for on casting our net from the bow, we caught several of that species, when the noise ceased for a time.

Nature, in her varied arrangements, seems to have felt a partiality toward this portion of our country. As the traveler ascends or descends the Ohio, he cannot help remarking that alternately, nearly the whole length of the river, the margin, on one side, is bounded by lofty hills and a rolling surface, while on the other, extensive plains of the

Audubon portrayed America's wildlife with pen as well as paintbrush. This account of a voyage down the Ohio is from his journal.

When my wife, my eldest son (then an infant), and myself were returning from Pennsylvania to Kentucky, we found it expedient, the waters being unusually low, to provide ourselves with a skiff, to enable us to proceed to our abode at Henderson. I purchased a large, commodious and light boat of that denomination. We procured a mattress, and our friends furnished us with ready prepared viands. We had two stout Negro rowers, and in this trim we left the village of Shippingport, in expectation of reaching the place of our destination in a very few days.

It was in the month of October, 1810. The autumnal tints already decorated the shores of that queen of rivers, the Ohio. Every tree was hung with long and flowing festoons of different species of vines, many loaded with clustered fruits of varied brilliancy, their rich bronzed carmine mingling beautifully with the yellow foliage, which now predominated over the yet green leaves, reflecting more lively and colorful tints from the clear stream richest alluvial land are seen as far as the eye can command the view. Islands of varied size and form rise here and there from the bosom of the water, and the winding course of the stream frequently brings you to places where the idea of being on a river of great length changes to that of floating on a lake of moderate extent. Some of these islands are of considerable size and value; while others, small and insignificant, seem as if intended for contrast, and as serving to enhance the general interest of the scenery. These little islands are frequently overflowed during great freshets or floods, and receive at their heads prodigious heaps of drifted timber. We foresaw with great concern the alterations that cultivation would soon produce along those delightful banks.

As night came, sinking in darkness the broader portions of the river, our minds became affected by strong emotions, and wandered far beyond the present moments. The tinkling of bells told us that the cattle which bore them were gently roving from valley to valley in search of food, or returning to their distant homes. The hooting of the Great Owl, or the muffled noise of its wings, as it sailed smoothly over the stream, were matters of interest to us; so was the sound of the boatman's horn, as it came winding more and more softly from afar. When daylight returned, many songsters burst forth with echoing notes, more and more mellow to the listening ear. Here and there the lone-

ly cabin of a squatter struck the eye, giving note of commencing civilization. The crossing of the stream by a deer foretold how soon the hills would be covered with snow.

Many sluggish flatboats we overtook and passed; some laden with produce from the different headwaters of the small rivers that pour their tributary streams into the Ohio; others, of less dimensions, crowded with emigrants from distant parts, in search of a new home. Purer pleasures I never felt; nor have you, reader, I ween, unless indeed you have felt the like, and in such company.

The margins of the shores and of the river were, at this season, amply supplied with game. A Wild Turkey, a Bluewinged Teal, or a Grouse, could be procured; and we fared very well, for, whenever we pleased, we landed, struck up a fire, and, provided as we were with the necessary utensils, had a good repast.

Audubon once kept a tame wild turkey as a pet. A red ribbon around its neck protected it from hunters—for a while.

When I think of these times, and call back to my mind the grandeur and beauty of those almost uninhabited shores; when I picture to myself the dense and lofty summits of the forests, that everywhere spread along the hills and overhung the margins of the stream, unmolested by the axe of the settler; when I know how dearly purchased the safe navigation of that river has been, by the blood of many worthy Virginians; when I see that no longer any aborigines are to be found there, and that the vast herds of Elk, Deer and Buffaloes which once pastured on these hills, and in these valleys, making for themselves great roads to the several salt-springs, have ceased to exist; when I reflect that all this grand portion of our Union, instead of being in a state of nature, is now more or less covered with villages, farms, and towns, where the din of hammers and machinery is constantly heard; that the woods are fast disappearing under the axe by day, and the fire by night; that hundreds of steamboats are gliding to and fro, over the whole length of the majestic river, forcing commerce to take root and to prosper at every spot; when I see the surplus population of Europe coming to assist in the destruction of the forest, and transplanting civilization into its darkest recesses; when I remember that these extraordinary changes have taken place in twenty years, I pause, wonder, and although I know all to be fact, can scarcely believe its reality.

Whether these changes are for the better or for the worse, I shall not pretend to say; but in whatever way my conclusions may incline, I feel with regret that there are on record no satisfactory accounts of the state of that portion of the country, from the time when our people first settled in it. This has not been because no one in America is able to accomplish such an undertaking. Our Irvings and our Coopers have proved themselves fully competent for the task. It has more probably been because the changes have succeeded each other with such rapidity as almost to rival the movements of their pens. *(1830)*

SPRING AT WALDEN POND
by Henry David Thoreau

In the morning I watched the geese from the door through the mist, sailing in the middle of the pond, fifty rods off, so large and tumultuous that Walden appeared like an artificial pond for their amusement. But when I stood on the shore they at once rose up with a great flapping of wings at the signal of their commander, and when they had got into ranks circled about over my head, twenty-nine of them, and then steered straight to Canada, with a regular *honk* from the leader at intervals, trusting to break their fast in muddier pools. A "plump" of ducks rose at the same time and took the route to the north in the wake of their noisier cousins.

For a week I heard the circling, groping clangor of some solitary goose in the foggy mornings, seeking its companion, and still peopling the woods with the sound of a larger life than they could sustain. In April the pigeons were seen again flying express in small flocks, and in due time I heard the martins twittering over my clearing, though it had not seemed that the township contained so many that it could afford me any, and I fancied that they were of the ancient race that dwelt in hollow trees ere white men came. In almost all climes the tortoise and the frog are among the precursors and heralds of this season, and birds fly with song and glancing plumage, and plants spring and bloom, and winds blow, to correct this slight oscillation of the poles and preserve the equilibrium of nature.

On the 29th of April, as I was fishing from the bank of the river near the Nine-Acre-Corner bridge, standing on the quaking grass and willow roots, where the muskrats lurk, I heard a singular rattling sound, somewhat like that of the sticks which boys will play with their fingers, when, looking up, I observed a very slight and graceful hawk, like a night-hawk, alternately

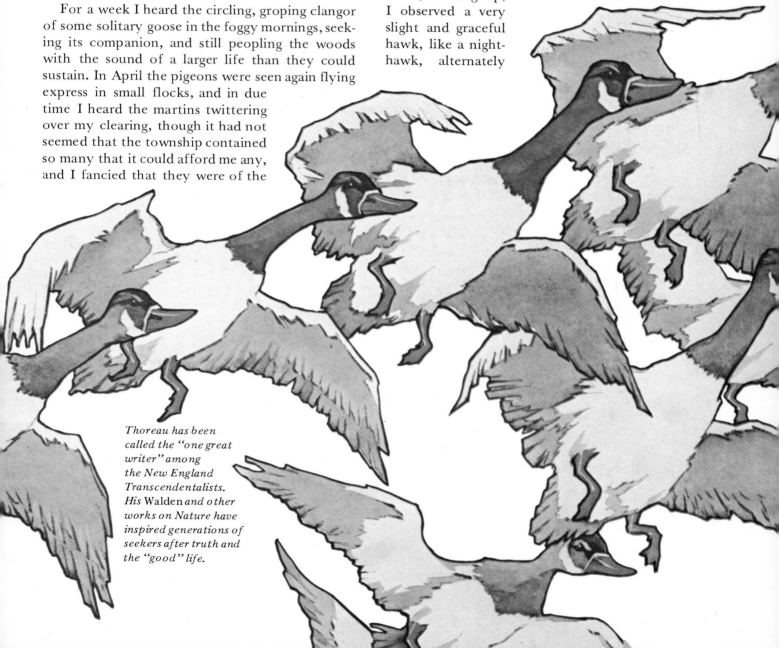

Thoreau has been called the "one great writer" among the New England Transcendentalists. His Walden *and other works on Nature have inspired generations of seekers after truth and the "good" life.*

soaring like a ripple and tumbling a rod or two over and over, showing the under side of its wings, which gleamed like satin ribbon in the sun, or like the pearly inside of a shell. This sight reminded me of falconry and what nobleness and poetry are associated with that sport. The merlin it seemed to me it might be called: but I care not for its name. It was the most ethereal flight I had ever witnessed. It did not simply flutter like a butterfly, nor soar like the larger hawks, but it sported with proud reliance in the fields of air; mounting again and again with its strange chuckle, it repeated its free and beautiful fall, turning over and over like a kite, and then recovering from its lofty tumbling, as if it had never set its foot on *terra firma*. It appeared to have no companion in the universe—sporting there alone—and to need none but the morning and the ether with which it played. It was not lonely, but made all the earth lonely beneath it. Where was the parent which hatched it, its kindred, and its father in the heavens? The tenant of the air, it seemed related to the earth but by an egg hatched sometime in the crevice of a crag—or was its native nest made in the angle of a cloud, woven of the rainbow's trimmings and the sunset sky, and lined with some soft midsummer haze caught up from earth? Its eyrie now some cliffy cloud.

Beside this I got a rare mess of golden and silver and bright cupreous fishes, which looked like a string of jewels. Ah! I have penetrated to those meadows on the morning of many a first spring day, jumping from hummock to hummock, from willow root to willow root, when the wild river valley and the woods were bathed in so pure and bright a light as would have waked the dead, if they had been slumbering in their graves, as some suppose. There needs no stronger proof of immortality. All things must live in such a light. O Death, where was thy sting? O Grave, where was thy victory, then?

Our village life would stagnate if it were not for the unexplored forests and meadows which surround it. We need the tonic of wildness—to wade sometimes in marshes where the bittern and the meadow-hen lurk, and hear the booming of the snipe; to smell the whispering sedge where only some wilder and more solitary fowl builds her nest, and the mink crawls with its belly close to the ground. At the same time that we are earnest to explore and learn all things, we require that all things be mysterious and unexplorable, that land and sea be infinitely wild, unsurveyed and unfathomed by us because unfathomable. We can never

have enough of Nature. We must be refreshed by the sight of inexhaustible vigor, vast and titanic features, the seacoast with its wrecks, the wilderness with its living and its decaying trees, the thundercloud, and the rain which lasts three weeks and produces freshets. We need to witness our own limits transgressed, and some life pasturing freely where we never wander. We are cheered when we observe the vulture feeding on the carrion which disgusts and disheartens us, and deriving health and strength from the repast. There was a dead horse in the hollow by the path to my house, which compelled me sometimes to go out of my way, especially in the night when the air was heavy, but the assurance it gave me of the strong appetite and inviolable health of Nature was my compensation for this. I love to see that Nature is so rife with life that myriads can be afforded to be sacrificed and suffered to prey on one another; that tender organizations can be so serenely squashed out of existence like pulp—tadpoles which herons gobble up, and tortoises and toads run over in the road; and that sometimes it has rained flesh and blood! With the liability to accident, we must see how little account is to be made of it. The impression made on a wise man is that of universal innocence. Poison is not poisonous after all, nor are any wounds fatal. Compassion is a very untenable ground. It must be expeditious. Its pleadings will not be stereotyped.

Early in May, the oaks, hickories, maples, and other trees, just putting out amidst the pine woods around the pond, imparted a brightness like sunshine to the landscape, especially in cloudy days, as if the sun were breaking through mists and shining faintly on the hillsides here and there. On the third or fourth of May I saw a loon in the pond, and during the first week of the month I heard the whippoorwill, the brown thrasher, the veery, the wood pewee, the chewink, and other birds. I had heard the wood thrush long before. The phoebe had already come once more and looked in at my door and window, to see if my house was cavernlike enough for her, sustaining herself on humming wings with clinched talons, as if she held by the air, while she surveyed the premises. The sulphur-like pollen of the pitch pine soon covered the pond and the stones and rotten wood along the shore, so that you could have collected a barrelful. This is the "sulphur showers" we hear of. Even in Calidas' drama of Sacontala, we read of "rills dyed yellow with the golden dust of the lotus." And so the seasons went rolling on into summer, as one rambles into higher and higher grass. *(1854)*

32

Spring's song is the high sweet piping of tree frog and peeper, transmuted by midsummer to the mellow bass of the bullfrog.

HE DRAWS GREAT LINES ACROSS THE SKY

by John Burroughs

The fox passes my door in winter, and probably in summer too, as do also the 'possum and the coon. The latter tears down my sweet corn in the garden, and the rabbit eats off my raspberry bushes and nibbles my first strawberries, while the woodchucks eat my celery and beans and peas. Chipmunks carry off the corn I put out for the chickens, and weasels eat the chickens themselves.

Many times during the season I have in my solitude a visit from the bald eagle. There is a dead tree near the summit, where he often perches, and which we call the "old eagle-tree." It is a pine, killed years ago by a thunderbolt—the bolt of Jove—and now the bird of Jove hovers about it or sits upon it. I have little doubt that what attracted me to this spot attracted him—the seclusion, the savageness, the elemental grandeur.

Sometimes, as I look out through my window early in the morning, I see the eagle upon his perch, preening his plumage, or waiting for the rising sun to gild the mountaintops. When the smoke begins to rise from my chimney, or he sees me going to the spring for water, he concludes it is time for him to be off. But he need not fear the crack of the rifle here; nothing more deadly than field glasses shall be pointed at him while I am about. Often in the course of the day I see him circling above my domain, or winging his way toward the mountains. His home is apparently in the Shawangunk Range, twenty or more miles distant, and I fancy he stops or lingers above me on his way to the river. The days on which I see him are not quite the same as the other days. I think my thoughts soar a little higher all the rest of the morning: I have had a visit from a messenger of Jove. The lift or range of those great wings has passed into my thought. I once heard a collector get up in a scientific body and tell how many eggs of the bald eagle he had clutched that season, how many from this nest, how many from that, and how one of the eagles had deported itself after he had killed its mate. I felt ashamed for him. He had only proved himself a superior human

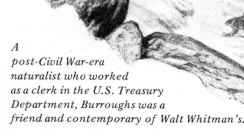

A post-Civil War-era naturalist who worked as a clerk in the U.S. Treasury Department, Burroughs was a friend and contemporary of Walt Whitman's.

weasel. The man with the rifle and the man with the collector's craze are fast reducing the number of eagles in the country. Twenty years ago I used to see a dozen or more along the river in the spring, where I now see only one or two, or none at all. What would it profit me could I find and plunder my eagle's nest, or strip his skin from his dead carcass? Should I know him better? I do not want to know him that way. I want rather to feel the inspiration of his presence and noble bearing. I want my interest and sympathy to go with him in his continental voyaging up and down, and in his long, elevated flights to and from his eyrie upon the remote, solitary cliffs. He draws great lines across the sky; he sees the forests like a carpet beneath him, he sees the hills and valleys as folds and wrinkles in a many-colored tapestry; he sees the river as a silver belt connecting remote horizons. We climb mountain peaks to get a glimpse of the spectacle that is hourly spread out beneath him. Dignity, elevation, repose are his. I would have my thoughts take as wide a sweep. I would be as far removed from the cares and turmoils of this noisy and blustering world. *(1886)*

Burroughs described the wildlife of the Catskills   *and Hudson River Valley.*

NATURE'S GARDENERS

by John Muir

Shortly after sunrise, just as the light was beginning to come streaming through the trees, while I lay leaning on my elbow taking my bread and tea, and looking down across the cañon, tracing the dip of the granite headlands, and trying to plan a way to the river at a point likely to be fordable, suddenly I caught the big bright eyes of a deer gazing at me through the garden hedge. The expressive eyes, the slim black-tipped muzzle and the large ears were as perfectly visible as if placed there at just the right distance to be seen, like a picture on a wall. She continued to gaze, while I gazed back with equal steadiness. In a few minutes she ventured forward a step, exposing her fine arching neck and forelegs, then snorted and withdrew.

This alone was a fine picture—the beautiful eyes framed in colored cherry leaves, the topmost sprays lightly atremble, and just glanced by the level sunrays, all the rest in shadow.

But more anon. Gaining confidence, and evidently piqued by curiosity, the trembling sprays indicated her return, and her head came into view; then another and another step, and she stood wholly exposed inside the garden hedge, gazed eagerly around, and again withdrew, but returned a moment afterward, this time advancing into the middle of the garden; and behind her I noticed a second pair of eyes, not fixed on me, but on her companion in front, as if eagerly questioning, "What in the world do you see?" Then more rustling in the hedge, and another head came slipping past the second, the two heads touching; while the first came within a few steps of me, walking with inimitable grace. My picture was being enriched and enlivened every minute; but even this was not all. After another timid little snort, as if testing my good intentions, all three disappeared; but I was true, and my wild beauties emerged once more, one, two, three, four, slipping through the dense hedge without snapping a twig, and all four came forward into the garden, moving, changing, lifting their smooth polished limbs with charming grace—the perfect embodiment of poetic form and motion. I have oftentimes remarked in meeting with deer that curiosity was sufficiently strong to carry them dangerously near hunters; but in this instance they seemed to have satisfied curiosity, and began to feel so much at ease in my company that they all began to feed in the garden—eating breakfast with me, like gentle sheep around a shepherd—while I observed keenly, to learn their gestures and what plants they fed on. They are the daintiest feeders I ever saw, and no wonder the Indians esteem the contents of their stomachs a great delicacy. They seldom eat grass, but chiefly aromatic shrubs. The Ceanothus and cherry seemed their favorites. They would cull a single cherry leaf with the utmost delicacy, then one of Ceanothus, now and then stalking across the garden to snip off a leaf or two of mint, their sharp muzzle enabling them to cull out the daintiest leaves one at a time. It was delightful to feel how perfectly the most timid wild animals may confide in man. They no longer required that I should remain motionless, taking no alarm when I shifted from one elbow to the other, and even allowed me to rise and stand erect.

It then occurred to me that I might possibly steal up to one of them and catch it, not with any intention of killing it, for that was far indeed from my thoughts. I only wanted to run my hand along its beautiful curving limbs. But no sooner had I made a little advance on this line than, giving a searching look, they bounded off with loud shrill snorts, vanishing in the forest. . . .

I have often tried to understand how so many deer, and wild sheep and bears, and flocks of grouse—nature's cattle and poultry—could be allowed to run at large through the mountain gardens without in any way marring their beauty. I was therefore all the more watchful of this feeding flock, and carefully examined the garden after they left, to see what flowers had suffered; but I could not detect the slightest disorder, much less destruction. It seemed rather that, like gardeners, they had been keeping it in order. At least I could not see a crushed flower, nor a single grass stem that was misbent or broken down. Nor among the daisy, gentian, Bryanthus gardens of the Alps, where the wild sheep roam at will, have I ever noticed the effects of destructive feeding or trampling. Even the burly shuffling bears beautify the ground on which they walk, picturing it with their awe-inspiring tracks, and also writing poetry on the soft sequoia bark in boldly drawn Gothic hieroglyphics. But, strange to say, man, the crown, the sequoia of nature, brings confusion with his gifts, and sweeps away the beauty of wildness like a fire. *(1878)*

36

Born in Scotland, Muir reached California in 1869, became the first naturalist to describe the wildlife and geological formations of the Yosemite Valley.

THE GAMES FOXES PLAY

by Ernest Thompson Seton

On May 15, 1882, as we drove over the prairie trail, my brother pointed to a yellow boulder some forty yards away on a hillside where were other boulders. "See," said he, doesn't that look like a fox?"

I replied: "No; I see nothing but a yellow boulder."

But his eyesight was much better than mine, and he persisted: "That's a fox curled up."

With our noisy wagon and team, we marched past, within thirty yards; then when twenty yards beyond, a puff of wind seemed to make a crack in the boulder.

"That certainly is a fox," said my brother. He stopped, turned, and took one step from the trail toward the "boulder," which at once sprang up and ran for its life. My brother was correct. A fox it was!

He skimmed across a stretch of burned black prairie; then, reaching a belt of unburned yellow grass 300 yards away, he crouched on this and watched us again; maybe because the grass was a good match for his own color, but more likely because it *was* cover.

I do not suppose he was asleep when first we saw him curled up among the boulders. He was probably watching us through his tail, trusting to his color; and would have lain still, hoping to escape our detection, had not my brother alarmed him by leaving the trail and venturing forth in his direction.

Each time, the significant fact seemed to be that the fox *knew* he resembled the boulder or the grass, and was willing to take advantage of that resemblance. . . .

Most animals drag their prey to cover. The clever fox tosses his onto his back so he can run fast, even with a heavy load.

The playful foxes romped basking in the warm sun, or wrestling with each other till a slight sound made them scurry underground. But their alarm was needless, for the cause of it was their mother; she stepped from the bushes bringing another hen—number seventeen as I remember. A low call from her and the little fellows came tumbling out. Then began a scene that I thought charming, but which my uncle would not have enjoyed at all.

They rushed on the hen, and tussled and fought with it, and each other, while the mother, keeping a sharp eye for enemies, looked on with fond delight. The expression on her face was quite remarkable.

It was first a grinning of delight, but her usual look of wildness and cunning was there, nor were cruelty and nervousness lacking, but over all was the unmistakable look of the mother's pride and love. . . .

This animal is not much given to social amusements, but Norton and Stevens both tell me that on their fur farms in Maine it is a common thing for the foxes to gather on moonlight nights and chase each other about with most uproarious barking and churring that do not seem to express anything but goodwill and hilarity.

This species uses the smell-telephone much less, I think, than the wolf does. Its principal method of intercommunication is doubtless by the voice. It has a short bark followed by a little squall like "*yap-yurr*." That is the sound oftenest uttered, but it has also a long yell and two or three different yowls or screeches as well as softer *churr-churrs* that doubtless have different meanings to its kind. The voice of the male is notably heavier and coarser than that of his mate. . . .

There is a device that I have several times known the Ontario fox to resort to when pressed by the hounds, that is, run along the railway ahead of a train, and cross a high trestle bridge. On one occasion I knew of a hound being thrown by the locomotive from the trestle into the river below, minus his tail, but otherwise unhurt. I was told, however, that all were not so fortunate, as some hounds had been killed at the same place in a similar way. It is very hard to say how much was intentional on the part of the fox. The fox-hunters who know the animal say *it was intentional throughout*. Some maintain that it was entirely accidental. It certainly was not necessary for the fox to know anything about train times, as he could hear the train coming miles away. The track is a notoriously bad place for scent to lie, the trestle was a place of difficult footing, like a sloping tree, which often furnishes refuge, or the steep sand bank already noted, where I several times saw the fox baffle the hounds. He might run to the train, just as I have known a deer

Born in England in 1860, Ernest Thompson Seton grew up in Canada, observing the wildlife of an area now part of Toronto. He wrote mostly the life stories of individual animals, all with tragic endings.

PAUL
BRANSON

39

The adversaries are not ill-matched, as the fox can usually outrun and outthink the much larger, heavier hounds.

or hare to run to a wagon or sleigh when flying for its life, preferring the unknown terror to the certain death. Add to this the element of luck when first the fox made the attempt; success that time would lead him to try again. . . .

No one can long watch a caged fox in wintertime without discerning the use to which it puts its great bushy tail. Its nose and pads are the only exposed parts, and those might easily be frostbitten when it sleeps during severe weather. But it is always careful on lying down to draw these together, then curl the brush around them; it acts both as wrap and respirator. I have many times seen wild ones do this same thing, and am satisfied that the tail is a neces-

sity to the fox, as well as to the squirrel and wolf. I believe a fox or coyote would die before spring if turned out in the autumn without a tail. . . .

My experiences with the Springfield (Ont.) fox (1888) gave me a large idea of the fox's sporty mind. Night after night, when I went prowling with my hound, not to hunt but to learn things, one of the foxes that lived nearby would give the dog a run. At first it seemed like the ordinary chances of the hunt, but I soon found that the fox would come to meet us if we were slow or late. Several times I sat down on a log to wait and listen, with the dog at my feet, when from the near woods sounded the tantalizing "Yap, yap" of the fox.

Away would go the dog in full cry, but the weather was hot and the scent poor, and soon the dog would come back panting to lie at my feet. Within three minutes the fox would announce his return by his yapping bark, coming nearer and barking more loudly, till the tired dog was led off on his fool's errand once more.

This game they played several times by daylight, and I had the pleasant experience of seeing how the dog was fooled when the fox wanted to get rid of him.

Reynard would lay his trail along a steep sandy cutbank that bordered the river. On dry sand, the scent is at all times poor, and in this case, the sand fell into his tracks so as apparently to destroy it altogether. At any rate, it was usually here that the dog lost it.

On one occasion, I was hidden within fifteen feet of that old dog-fox, as he sat on his haunches to watch the dog vainly looking for the trail on this bank, the fox grinning to his ears as the dog went searching about. He not only grinned, but, though quite unwinded, he uttered a loud panting noise that surely was a fox laugh. In his eagerness to see the result of his trick-trailing, he several times stood up on his hind legs. I never had any question of a fox's sense of humor after what I saw on those occasions.

To the hunter he is both competitor and quarry; to the farmer he is a nocturnal thief who raids henhouse and rabbit hutch.
Every man's hand is raised against him, and suburban sprawl robs him of his hiding places. Yet by his wits he survives.

THE WEST WAS A SEA OF GRASS
by Chet Huntley

TV newsman Huntley, son of homesteaders, first saw Montana's grasslands from the seat of a jouncing spring wagon in 1916. By then the great buffalo herds were gone, but they had left their mark on the "big sky" country Huntley learned to love.

Wind and grass in assonant conversation. The grass . . . the incredible grass! In March it was only the dried remains of the last year's growth, which had borne up and withstood the crushing weight of the winter snow. Indeed, it had carried the weight of the snow crop like a forest of supporting beams and pillars. In places the snow might come only within proximity of the earth, and as it melted, the drops of water trickled down the myriad stems and blades. Then the dead stalks, free of encumbrance, performed their ballet to the wind, before succumbing, as nutrient, to the rush of new growth surging up from the burgeoning soil.

"Buffalo grass" (*Buchloe dactyloides*) it was called, and it had been host to the tremendous herds which had thrived on the broad plateau rolling gently upward and northward from the Milk River, across the Canadian border, and a hundred miles or so into Alberta, Saskatchewan and Manitoba. From east to west, the grass ocean stretched undulating from the base of the Canadian and Montana Rockies, across North Dakota and the lower halves of the Canadian provinces to the fringe of the Minnesota-Manitoba lake country.

From every spring or creek, from every swale and gully where the snow water collected and remained through the hot summers, thousands of buffalo trails radiated out toward the endless pasture land. Millions of sharp hooves had cut deep paths into the earth and carved terraces on the hillsides. A hundred years of domestic grazing, cultivation, and the consequent intensified erosion by wind and water, would not erase the marks which the great beasts had left upon their land.

The buffalo was a restrained and gentle user of the land and the grass . . . his grass, upon which the incredible growth and development of the herds depended. He ate it sparingly, grazing off only the tops of the stems, which grew as high as his magnificent head. The tops of the tender stalks contained the seedlings, the flavored nut, the storehouse of protein, and they waved there at the level of his maw. It was a reciprocal balance of favor. The buffalo spared the grass roots and left most of the stem for the protection of the new growth. In return, the grass replenished and fed upon itself in a perpetual cycle of abundance.

The great herds had vanished, but not so long ago. Thirty years earlier, there had been a few remnant groups scattered through the Milk River plateau and hidden in the lower folds of the Little Rockies. All over that vast expanse the carcasses and the frequent mounds of bleaching bones gave mute testimony to the destructive efficiency of man. Even the herds of the Milk River country, sometimes filling the horizons, could not endure the slaughter. By pack train, barge or wagon, mountains of hides had been carried to Williston or Mandan and then by flatboat down the Missouri to the leather factories of St. Louis. No respectable carriage in all America was wanting its buffalo robes. Nor was there anyone to suggest cropping the buffalo with specified kills each year. Americans were preoccupied with the squandering of their inheritance, and they went about it with energy and dispatch.

So the land had been left to the grass and its smaller denizens. The grass thrived and grew taller, forming an endless sea of seasonal green and gold; and in winter, it rose out of the snow to relieve the white monotony. Each blade and each stem, in consort with the winds sweeping down from the Canadian Northwest, sculptured on the snow surface its own minute drift, frosting the winterland with lacy musings of bas relief.   *(1968)*

42

In little more than 100 years man has changed irrevocably the landscape of the American West.

WE ARE SLOW TO LEARN

by John Steinbeck

I have often wondered at the thoughtlessness and savagery with which our early settlers approached this enormously rich continent. They came at it as if it were an enemy, which of course it was. They burned the forests, they swept the buffalo from the plains, blasted the streams, and ran a reckless scythe through the virgin and noble timber.

Perhaps they felt that the land could never be exhausted, that a man could move on to new wonders endlessly. They pillaged the country as though they hated it, as though they held it temporarily and might be driven off at any time.

This tendency toward irresponsibility persists in very many of us today— our rivers are poisoned by reckless dumping of sewage and toxic industrial wastes, the air of our cities is filthy and dangerous to breathe from the belching of uncontrolled products from combustion of coal, coke, oil and gasoline. Our towns are girdled with wreckage and the debris of our toys— our automobiles and our packaged pleasures.

Through our uninhibited spraying against one enemy we have destroyed the natural balances our survival requires. All of these evils can and must be overcome if America and the Americans are to survive; but a great many of us still conduct ourselves as our ancestors did, stealing from the future for our clear and present profit.

Since the river polluters, the air poisoners are not criminal or even bad people, we must presume that they are heirs to the early conviction that sky and water are unowned and that they are limitless. In the light of our practices here at home it is interesting to read of the care taken with the carriers of our probes into space, to make utterly sure that they are free of pollution of any kind. We would not think of doing to the moon what we do every day to our own country.

When the first settlers came to America and dug in on the coast, they huddled in defending villages hemmed in by the sea on one side and by endless forests on the other, by Red Indians and, most frightening, the mystery of an unknown land extending nobody knew how far. And for a time very few cared or dared to find out.

Later, however, brave and forest-wise men drifted westward to hunt, to trap, and eventually to bargain for the furs which were the first negotiable wealth America produced for trade and export. Then trading posts were set up as centers of collection, and the exploring men moved up and down the rivers and crossed the mountains, made friends for mutual profit with the Indians, learned the wilderness techniques, so that these explorer-traders soon dressed, ate, and generally acted like the indigenous people around them.

For a goodly time the Americans were travelers moving about the country collecting its valuables, but with little idea of permanence; their roots and their hearts were in the towns and the growing cities along the eastern edge. Then the population began to move westward. The newcomers were of peasant stock, and they had their roots in a Europe where they had been landless, for the possession of land was the requirement for and the proof of a higher social class than they had known. In America they found beautiful and boundless land for the taking—and they took it. They cut and burned the forests to make room for crops, and when they had cropped out a piece they moved on, raping the country like invaders. The topsoil, held by roots and freshened by leaf-fall, was left helpless to the spring freshets, stripped and eroded with the naked bones of clay and rock exposed.

The merciless 19th century was like a hostile expedition for loot that seemed limitless. Buffalo by the thousands were killed, stripped of their hides, and left to rot, a reservoir of permanent food supply eliminated. More than that, the land of the Great Plains was robbed forever of the manure of the herds. Then the settlers' plows went in and ripped off the protection of the buffalo grass and opened the helpless soil to quick water and slow drought and the mischievous winds that roamed through the Great Central Plains. There has always been more than enough desert in America; the swarms of new settlers, like overindulged children, created even more desert. They moved like locusts across the continent until the western sea put a boundary to their movements.

An aroused and fearful government made laws for the distribution of public lands—a quarter section, 160 acres, per person—and a claim had to be proved and improved; but there were ways of getting around this, and legally. . . . One joker with a name still remembered in the West worked out a scheme copied many times in later years. Proving a quarter section required a year of residence and some kind of improvement—a fence, a shack—but once the land was proved, the owner was free to sell it. This particular princely character went to the skid row of the towns and found a small army of hopeless alcoholics who lived for whiskey and nothing else. He put these men on land he wanted to own, grub-staked them and kept them in cheap liquor until the acreage was proved, then went through the motions of buying it from his proteges and moved them and their one-room shacks on sled runners on to new quarter sections. Bums of strong constitution might prove out five or six homesteads for this acquisitive hero before they died of drunkenness.

It was full late when we began to realize that the continent did not stretch out to infinity; that there were limits to the indignities to which we could subject it. Conservation came to us slowly, and much of it hasn't arrived yet. We are slow to learn, but we do learn. From early times we were impressed and awed by the fantastic accidents of nature, like the Grand Canyon and Yosemite and Yellowstone Park. The Indians had revered them as holy places, visited by the gods, and all of us came to have somewhat the same feeling about them. Thus, as the feeling of preciousness of the things we had been destroying grew in Americans, we set aside more and more areas as national and state parks—to be looked at but not injured. And we no longer believe that a man, by owning a piece of America, is free to outrage it. *(1966)*

WHEN THE WORLD WAS STILL YOUNG

TALES FROM AROUND THE WORLD

The Woman Who Raised a Bear as Her Son

North America (Eskimo)

There was once an old woman who lived by herself in a small igloo near the seashore. She had no family, but she was a kindly woman, and the Eskimos who lived nearby were fond of her and brought her food.

One day, a hunter's wife came to her igloo and called through the doorway, "Dear little woman, would you like to have a polar bear cub? My children found him in the snow."

The old woman carried the little snow-white cub into her house. The tiny bear shivered with cold, and the woman cuddled him to keep him warm. She fed him roasted whale blubber, for she had heard that bears liked blubber. Soon the cub became lively and playful. From that time on, she gave him blubber to eat and melted blubber to drink. At night, the little cub lay beside her, tucked under the warm reindeer-skin blankets.

The old woman looked after the bear cub as though he were her own child, and he grew healthy and strong. She talked to the cub in the Eskimo language, and the bear learned to understand her.

The old woman was no longer lonely, and the Eskimos who lived nearby brought her food for the little cub. Even the children came to her igloo and called out, "Little bear, come out and play with us."

Then the old woman would say, "Little bear, remember to cover your claws when you play with children."

Sometimes, when the bear played with the children, he broke their toy harpoons to pieces. But whenever the bear wrestled with them, or played tag, he always covered his claws.

The Eskimo depends entirely on animals for food, clothing, fuel.

In the following months the little polar bear cub grew strong and brave. Then, one day at dawn, village hunters came to the old woman's window and called, "Little bear, come hunting with us. You may help us find a seal and earn a share of our catch."

And the bear went hunting with the men.

When the men returned home that night, they told the old woman, "Your bear is a wonderful hunter. But he was nearly killed by villagers from the north who mistook him for a wild bear. Give him some mark so that we can easily recognize him."

So the old woman made a mark for him to wear. She made a collar of plaited sealskin, as broad as a harpoon line.

After that, men always invited their friend the polar bear to hunt with them. He grew stronger than the strongest Eskimo hunters. He even hunted in the worst weather, when no Eskimo dared leave his igloo. He brought seals for the old woman to eat, and she shared her food with her neighbors. People in many other villages learned about the friendly bear, and recognized him by his collar. But in one of the villages, there was an evil man who said, "If I ever see the bear with the collar, I will kill him."

One day, the old woman said to the bear, "Whenever you meet Eskimo hunters, treat them as if you were one of them. Never harm them unless they attack you first."

The white bear listened to the old woman's words.

And so the old woman kept the bear with her. In the summer he hunted in the sea, and in the winter on the ice. The Eskimo hunters learned to know his ways and the bear shared his catch when the weather was so bad that no man dared venture out.

One day during a storm, the bear was away hunting and did not come home until evening. He entered the igloo slowly and sadly, and lay down on his bed. The old woman was alarmed and stepped out of the igloo for a moment, and found the body of a man. She hurried to the nearest house, and cried at the door, "Please help me! my little bear has come home with a dead man!"

When it grew light, the people went out and saw that it was the man from the north who said that he would kill the bear if he ever saw him. Afterwards, they heard from other hunters that the man had attacked the bear, and would not leave him alone.

After this had happened, the old woman said to the bear, "Someday soon, that evil man's sons will try to kill you. You had better leave me."

She wept as she said it. And the bear lay down on the floor and wept too.

The next morning the old woman said, "My sweet little bear, now you had better go."

When the bear was ready to leave, the old woman, weeping sadly, dipped her hands in black oil and

In Eskimo folktales the animals are friends and benefactors, as in this story, or powerful gods to whom offerings must be made.

stroked the sides of the white bear's head. The bear sniffed at her and went away toward the hills of snow and ice. The old woman cried all that day, and her friends also mourned the loss of their friend.

Men say that, far to the north, they sometimes see a huge bear with a black spot on each side of his head. Although he is a fierce and excellent hunter, he has never been known to harm a man.

Why There's Death in the World

Africa

Long, long ago, when God created the world, he promised that there would be no death at all. People would grow old, but they would be very wise and strong in their old age.

When God wanted to send this message to the world he chose the dog and the tortoise to be his messengers.

"Go," God said, "and tell all the people that I have created that there will be no sickness and no death on the earth!"

God repeated this message twice. Dog wagged his tail and Tortoise nodded his head.

The tortoise knew that he was very slow, so while Dog was still dancing about and wagging his tail Tortoise started walking to earth.

He repeated God's message at every step he took. As he raised his left front foot, he said "O-um" and as he put it down he said "Death." Then he dragged his body forward and raised his right foot saying "O-um" and put it down saying "Sickness." So Tortoise moved slowly and slowly and slowly on, singing:

> "O-um death . . . O-um sickness
> O-um death . . . O-um sickness
> O-um death . . . O-um sickness."

By the time Dog stopped dancing, Tortoise was far ahead, dragging himself slowly and slowly and slowly down to earth. Dog ran after him—

> Vugu, vugu
> Vugu, vugu
> Vugu, vugu

cutting through the wind like a racehorse. When he slowed down, he saw Tortoise far behind, still singing "O-um death . . . O-um sickness."

Tortoise was so far behind that Dog decided to nose about for a bone in a heap of rubbish beside the path. He nosed and he nosed and he nosed and he finally found a bone. He sat down crunching his bone. You could have heard him crunching—

> Kraun, kraun, kraun, kraun!

All the time Tortoise was plodding on with his message, "O-um . . . O-um . . . O-um." Dog was still eating when he saw Tortoise ahead of him again. Bone in his mouth, he started to run—

> Vugu, vugu
> Vugu, vugu

and before you could wink your eye and say "Mako!" Dog had gone past Tortoise again. Twice he dropped his bone and twice he stopped to grab it from the ground. The third time Tortoise was so far behind that Dog went into the bush, lay down in the cool shade of a tree, and started crunching the bone again. He was munching so loudly that the people on earth could hear him—

> Kraun, kraun, kraun, kraun!

Tortoise was still walking. He never stopped. He never gave up. He never forgot his "O-um death . . . O-um sickness."

You could see his front feet going up and down, first his left foot, then his right. Every time he would raise his head and bow, raise and bow, and every time he would say:

> "O-um death! from God to man
> O-um sickness! from God to man
> O-um death! from God to man
> O-um sickness! from God to man!"

Dog came out of the bush feeling very satisfied and strong and off he ran after the tortoise—

> Vugu, vugu, vugu, vugu
> Vugu, vugu, vugu, vugu
> Vugu, vugu, vugu, vugu
> Vugu, vugu, vugu, vugu!

Before you could wink your eye and say "Mako!" he had run past the struggling tortoise.

But by now the sun was very hot. Dog was so thirsty he felt as if there were an oven in his throat. Tortoise was far behind again so with a scornful laugh Dog went into the bush to look for a stream and drink some water.

Tortoise still plodded on. At every breath he would repeat his message and make his bow. But his voice was growing weaker and weaker. By the time Dog came out of the bush, refreshed and strong, he saw Tortoise far ahead with a crowd of people.

Tortoise felt so faint and tired he could only pant the few words he still remembered of God's message to the people. All he could say was:

"Death . . . sickness,
God . . . to man."

He went on announcing that God had said there would be death and sickness, death and sickness.

Dog came racing up too late. Tortoise had already delivered his message twice, and no one, not even God, could change it. Poor Dog began to cry. When the people asked him why he was crying, he said that Tortoise's message was wrong. God had said there would be *no* death and *no* sickness in the world.

The people were angry. They knew that Dog had come too late and the message could not be changed. So they told Dog that as long as death and sickness were in the world he would always be found nosing along the roadside looking for food and crunching on old dry bones.

Why the Pike Takes the Hook

Russia

On the eve of Ivanov Day (which is the day of Saint John and Midsummer as well) there was born the pike, a huge fish, with such teeth as never were. And when the pike was born the waters of the river foamed and raged, so that the ships in the river were all but swamped, and the pretty young girls who were playing on the banks ran away as fast as they could, frightened, they were, by the roaring of the waves, and the black wind and the white foam on the water. Terrible was the birth of the sharp-toothed pike.

And when the pike was born he did not grow up by months or by days, but by hours. Every day it was two inches longer than the day before. In a month it was two yards long; in two months it was twelve feet long; in three months it was raging up and down the river like a tempest, eating the bream and the perch, and all the small fish that came in its way. There was a bream or a perch swimming lazily in the stream. The pike saw it as it raged by, caught it in its great white mouth, and instantly the bream or the perch was gone, torn to pieces by the pike's teeth, and swallowed as you would swallow a sunflower seed. And bream and perch are big fish. It was worse for the little ones.

What was to be done? The bream and the perch put their heads together in a quiet pool. It was clear enough that the great pike would eat every one of them. So they called a meeting of all the little fish, and set to thinking what could be done by way of dealing with the great pike, which had such sharp teeth and was making so free with their lives.

They all came to the meeting—bream, and perch, and roach, and dace, and gudgeon; yes, and the little yersh with his spiny back.

The silly roach said, "Let us kill the pike."

But the gudgeon looked at him with his great eyes, and asked, "Have you got good teeth?"

"No," says the roach, "I haven't any teeth."

"You'd swallow the pike," says the perch.

"My mouth is too small."

"Then do not use it to talk foolishness," said the gudgeon; and the roach's fins blushed scarlet, and are red to this day.

"I will set my prickles on end," says the perch, who has a row of sharp prickles in the fin on his back. "The pike won't find them too comfortable in his throat."

"Yes," said the bream, "but you will have to go into his throat to put them there, and he'll swallow you all the same."

There was a lot more foolishness talked. Even the minnows had something to say, until they were made to be quiet by the dace.

Now the little yersh had come to the meeting, with his spiny back, and his big front fins, and his head all shining in blue and gold and green. And when he had heard all, he began to talk.

"Think away," says he, "and break your heads, and spoil your brains, if ever you had any; but listen for a moment to what I have to say."

And all the fish turned to listen to the yersh, who is the cleverest of all the little fish, because he has a big head and a small body.

"Listen," says the yersh. "It is clear enough that the pike lives in this big river, and that he does not give the little fish a chance, crunches them all with his sharp teeth, and swallows them ten at a time. I quite agree that it would be much better for everybody if he could be killed; but not one of us is strong enough for that. We are not strong enough to kill him; but we can starve him, and save ourselves at the same time. There's no living in the big river while he is here. Let all us little fish clear out, and go and live in the little rivers that flow into the big. There the waters are shallow, and we can hide among the weeds. No one will touch us there, and we can live and bring up our children in peace, and only be in danger when we go visiting from one little river to another. And as for the great pike, we will leave him alone in the big river to rage hungrily up and down. His teeth will soon grow blunt, for there will be nothing for him to eat."

All the little fish waved their fins and danced in the water when they heard the wisdom of the yersh's speech. And the yersh and the roach, and the bream and the perch, and the dace and the gudgeon left the big river and swam up the little rivers between the green meadows. And there they began again to live in peace and bring up their little ones, though the cunning fishermen set nets in the little rivers and caught many of them on their way. From that time on there have never been many little fish in the big river.

And as for the monstrous pike, he swam up and down the great river, lashing the waters, and driving his nose through the waves, but found no food for his sharp teeth. He had to take to worms, and was caught in the end on a fisherman's hook. Yes, and the fisherman made soup of him—the best fish soup that ever was made. He was a friend of mine when I was a boy, and he gave me a taste in my wooden spoon.

The Man Who Turned into a Tiger

China

Chang Feng was traveling in the Fukien province in the beginning of Yuanho's reign (806-820). He was a northerner, and the luxuriant subtropical vegetation was new and interesting to him. Among other things, he had heard of tigers in the south. One day he was stopping with his servant at an inn in Hengshan, a small town near Foochow, lying on the watershed of the high mountain ranges which divide Fukien from Chekiang. Having deposited his luggage, he went out to take in his first impressions of the land, its people and the women's costumes. Walking alone with a cane in his hand, he went on and on, attracted by the refreshing green of the country after rain, and the bracing winds which came over the mountain. He felt strangely excited. Before him lay a landscape which was a riotous display of colors. It was autumn and the hillsides literally glowed with the gold and red of maple forests. A beautiful white temple stood halfway up the mountain above a thickly wooded slope. The golden sunset transformed the mountainside and the fields into a landscape of brilliant pastels, blue and purple and green, changing in hue at every moment, mingling with the dazzling red and gold. It was like a magic land.

Suddenly he felt a fainting sensation: stars danced before his eyes and his head reeled. He thought it was due to the altitude, the overexertion, and the sudden change of climate, or perhaps he was affected by the strange light. Just a few steps before him he saw a pasture land covered with velvety lawn, lying just where the wooded slope began. He took off his gown and put it with his walking stick against a tree, and lay down to take a rest. He felt a little better. As he looked up at the blue sky, he thought how beautiful and peaceful nature was. Men fought for money and position and fame; they lied and cheated and killed for gain; but here was peace—in nature. As he rolled in the grass, he felt happy and relaxed. The smell of the sod and of a gentle breeze soon caressed him into sleep.

When he woke up, he felt hungry and remembered it was evening. As he rolled his hands over his stomach, he touched a coating of soft fur. Quickly he sat up, and he saw his body covered with beautiful black stripes, and as he stretched his arms, he felt a delightful new strength in them, sinewy and full of power. He yawned and was surprised at his own powerful roar.

The deceptively serene landscape of legend conceals terror.

Looking down his own face, he saw the tips of long white whiskers. Lo, he had been transformed into a tiger!

Now, that is delightful, he thought to himself. I am no longer a man, but a tiger. It is not bad for a change.

Wanting to try his new strength, he raced to the forest and bounced from rock to rock, delighting in his new strength. He went up to the monastery, and pawed at the gate, seeking admittance.

"It is a tiger!" he heard a monk inside shouting. "I smell it. Do not open!"

Now that is uncomfortable, he thought to himself. I only intended to have a simple supper and discuss Buddhist philosophy with him. But of course I am a tiger now, and perhaps I do smell.

He had an instinct that he should go down the hill to the village and seek for food. As he hid behind a hedge on a country path, he saw a beautiful girl passing close by, and he thought to himself, I have been told that Foochow girls are famous for their white complexion and small stature. Indeed it is true.

As he made a move to go up to the girl, she screamed and ran away as fast as her legs would carry her.

What kind of a life is this, when everybody takes you for an enemy? he wondered. I will not eat her, she is so beautiful. I will take a pig, if I can find one.

At the thought of a nice, fat pig, or a small juicy lamb, his mouth watered, and he felt ashamed of himself. But there was this infernal hunger gnawing at his stomach, and he knew he had to eat something or die. He searched the village for a pig or calf, or even a chicken, but they were all under good shelters. All doors were shut against him, and as he crouched in a dark alley, waiting for a stray animal, he heard people talking inside their houses about a tiger in the village.

Unable to satisfy his hunger, he went back to the mountain, and lay in wait for some wayfarer in the night. All night he waited, but nothing came his way. For a while, he must have fallen asleep.

Toward dawn, he woke up. Soon travelers began to pass along the mountain road. He saw a man coming up from the city who stopped several passengers to ask whether they had seen Cheng Chiu, a bureau chief of Foochow, who was expected to return to his office today. He was evidently a clerk from the bureau who had been sent to welcome the chief.

Something told the tiger that he must eat Cheng Chiu. Just why he must eat that person he could not tell, but the feeling was very definite that Cheng Chiu was destined to be his first victim. He crouched in a thicket and waited for his victim.

Soon he saw Cheng Chiu coming up the road with his secretaries, along with a group of other travelers. Cheng looked fat and juicy and delicious. When Cheng Chiu came within pouncing distance, the tiger, Chang, rushed out, felled him to the ground, and carried him up the mountain. The travelers were so frightened they all ran away. Chang's hunger was satisfied, and he only felt as if he had had a bigger breakfast than usual. He finished up the gentleman and left only the hair and bones.

Satisfied with his meal, he lay down to take a nap. When he woke up, he thought he must have been mad to eat a human being who had done him no harm. His head cleared and he decided it was not such a pleasant life, prowling night after night for food. He remembered the night before, when the instinct of hunger drove him to the village and up the mountain, and he could do nothing to stop himself.

"Why do I not go back to that lawn and see if I can become a human being again?"

He found the spot where his clothing and walking stick were still lying by the tree. He lay down again, with the wish that he might wake up to be a man once more. He rolled over on the grass, and in a few seconds found that he had been restored to his human shape.

Greatly delighted, but puzzled by the strange experience, he put on his gown, took up his cane, and started back to the town. When he reached the inn, he found he had been away exactly twenty-four hours.

"Where have you been, Master?" asked his servant. "I have been out looking for you all day." The innkeeper also came up to speak to him, evidently relieved to see him return.

"We have been worried about you," said the innkeeper. "There was a tiger abroad. He was seen by a girl in the village last night, and this morning Cheng Chiu, a bureau chief who was returning to his office, was eaten by him."

Chang Feng made up a story that he had spent the night discussing Buddhist philosophy up in the temple.

"You are lucky!" cried the innkeeper, shaking his head. "It was in that neighborhood that Cheng Chiu was killed by the tiger."

"No, the tiger will not eat me," Chang Feng replied.

"Why not?"

"He cannot," said Chang Feng enigmatically.

Chang Feng kept the secret to himself, for he could not afford to tell anybody that he had eaten a man. It would be embarrassing, to say the least.

He went back to his home in Honan, and a few years went by. One day he was stopping at Huaiyang, a city on the Huai River. His friends gave him a dinner and much wine was consumed, as was usual on such occasions. Between the courses and the sipping of wine, the guests were each asked to tell a strange experience, and if in the opinion of the company the story was not strange enough, the teller of the story was to be fined a cup of wine.

Chang Feng began to tell his own story, and it happened that one of the guests was the son of Cheng Chiu, the man he had eaten. As he proceeded with his story, the young man's face grew angrier and angrier.

"So it was you who killed my father!" the young man shouted at him, his eyes distended and the veins standing up on his temples.

Chang Feng hastily stood up and apologized. He knew he had got into a very serious situation. "I am sorry. I did not know it was your father."

The young man suddenly whipped out a knife and threw it at him. Luckily it missed.

"I will kill you to avenge my father's death. I will follow you to the ends of the earth!" the young man shouted.

The friends persuaded Chang Feng to leave the house at once and hide himself for a while, while

Only in old tales is the tiger a menace to the Chinese. The big cat is extinct throughout most of its range and there are probably only about 2,500 alive today, counting those in zoos.

they tried to calm Cheng Chiu's son. It was conceded by everybody that to avenge one's father's death was a noble and laudable undertaking, but after all, Chang Feng had eaten Cheng Chiu when he was a tiger, and no one wanted to see more blood shed. It was a novel situation and posed a complicated moral problem as to whether revenge under such circumstances was justified. The youth still swore murder to appease his father's spirit.

In the end, the friends spoke to the commander of the region who ordered the young man to cross the Huai River and never return to the northern bank, while Chang Feng changed his name and went to the northwest to keep as far away from his sworn enemy as possible.

When the young man returned to his home, his friends said to him, "We entirely sympathize with your determination to avenge your father. That is a son's duty, of course. However, Chang Feng ate your father when he was a tiger and not responsible for his action. He did not know your father and had no purpose in killing him. That was a strange and special case, but it was not intentional murder, and if you kill him, you will be tried for murder."

The son respected this advice and did not pursue Chang Feng anymore.

55

How the Duck Got His Bill

North America
(Indian)

There was once a marriage feast. A mallard duck gave the feast, for it was she who was married, and she gave the feast in her camp. All the ducks were invited, and they came, from their camps by the lake, from their camps beyond the lake. The ducks came and the feast was spread out for them.

Whatever was good was provided: fish and mussels and salmon. Whatever was served was good, and the guests praised it. Above all, they praised the spoons the new husband had made, for never before had the ducks seen such things.

The spoons were made of horn, hard and tough, but not too hard, brown-colored, yet with yellow through the brown. They were long and flat, not too long, not too flat, rounded just right.

'They were exactly right," the ducks said. "Exactly right for eating," the admiring ducks said, the spoons.

Slightly smaller than the mallard, crested and more colorful, the wood duck nests high in a hollow tree.

So the feast was finished and the marriage songs were sung, and when everything was done, the ducks went home. And each duck took his spoon with him.

The ducks kept the spoons from the feasts. They gave them to their children and their children's children. The ducks still have their spoons. They take them wherever they go. Each duck has his spoon fastened to the end of his nose, so that he will not lose it or leave it behind.

Why the Bear is Stumpy-Tailed

Norway

One day the Bear met the Fox, who came slinking along with a string of fish he had stolen.

"Whence did you get those?" asked the Bear.

"Oh! my Lord Bruin, I've been out fishing and caught them," said the Fox.

So the Bear had a mind to learn to fish too, and bade the Fox tell him how he was to set about it.

"Oh! it's an easy craft for you," answered the Fox, "and soon learnt. You've only got to go upon the ice, and cut a hole and stick your tail down into it; and so you must go on holding it there as long as you can. You're not to mind if your tail smarts a little; that's when the fish bite. The longer you hold it there the more fish you'll get; and then all at once out with it, with a cross pull sideways, and with a strong pull too."

Yes; the Bear did as the Fox had said, and held his tail a long, long time down in the hole, till it was fast frozen in. Then he pulled it out with a cross pull, and it snapped short off.

That's why Bruin goes about with a stumpy tail this very day.

The Jaguar and the Goat

South America

Up in the sky, the sun was shining brightly through a narrow break in a dark sea of clouds banked above the wooded hilltops, and the goat Cavaramacho was cropping the grass that grew green among the crags. When the storm drew a curtain before the sun, preliminary to hurling lightning and thunder from its gloomy depths over the trembling earth and flaming heights, the goat was overcome by panic and started running over the steep slopes until the dark mouth of a cave bearded with weeds opened before him and he slipped rashly in.

Carried away by his frenzied impulse, Cavaramacho penetrated to the rear of the grotto; there he stopped, his flanks shaking with nervous terror. But soon, as his eyes became accustomed to the dark, he saw with unabated horror a fearful personage quietly resting within the cave, and at the same time dominating its entrance. The personage was watching him with the calm indifference which comes from strength and a sense of security.

Faced with the unforeseen but real danger into which he had fallen by fleeing from an imaginary one, Cavaramacho feverishly racked his brain as to how to save his life, unquestionably threatened by Yaguarete, the terrible jaguar, who was thus unexpectedly provided with his day's meal.

The goat, drawing strength from weakness, began to paw the hard floor of the cave, breathing heavily every now and then with his head down, hiding his curly beard and exhibiting the whole ominous length of his curved horns.

The jaguar, stretched on the ground with his short stout forelegs in front of him, calmly watched the extravagant animal, a relative of the deer, whose unusual actions he could not understand and whose presence had not yet awakened his appetite, sated by a recent meal. He watched him fixedly with half-shut eyes whose yellow pupils gleamed softly, and subconsciously he considered keeping for dinner the unexpected visitor, so well nourished on the fragrant herbs of the mountain slopes.

In the midst of his pacing up and down, Cavaramacho suddenly appeared to notice the presence of Yaguarete, and, pretending a certain agreeable surprise, he greeted him with an affectedly humorous and waggish air.

"Hello! So you've been here all along? I ought to have guessed it by your scent if by nothing else."

And he raised his head, the unwonted brilliance of his eyes and the formidable aspect of his horns and his quivering beard partly masking his terror.

"Yes, I am here," asserted Yaguarete, "and it is quite possible that you did not know of my presence because your own scent was so strong."

And gazing fixedly at the goat while licking himself quietly with his pink tongue, he added: "And what were you looking for in my house?"

"Looking for? Why, nothing," answered Cavaramacho, blinking before the great cat's searching glance. "I was strolling through these hills, gorging myself on grass and herbs— whose virtues keep my incomparable strength and daring— when I decided, suddenly and without deliberate intention of bothering you, to enter this pleasant refuge to escape the

consequences of a sudden downpour which might have dimmed the brilliance of my lovely coat. Wasn't that all right?"

"Ah, splendid!" replied the jaguar, with the inner intention of amusing himself for a while with the picturesque creature whose exaggerated airs and posturing did not alarm him. "And how do you spend your idle time after you have eaten your fill of herbs?" he added.

"In hunting, of course."

"Ah, magnificent! We are fellow-huntsmen, then."

"Only up to a certain point. I go hunting for the pure sport of the thing, for I find it repugnant to eat the flesh I have mutilated by my sharp horns. That is where I differ from men, who organize the hunts to sate their appetites and have to be urged on by hunger or famine before they face danger. I should be happy to think that your fearlessness and hero-

ism are not like men's in that respect. And I go hunting," the goat continued, "only to keep my courage in training. For food, I have grass, herbs, and numberless flowers and fruits, which I prefer to the palpitating flesh of my fellow creatures. Don't you prefer, for example, a branch heavily laden with sweet fruits to the neck of a pig?"

The jaguar was becoming interested, but without answering Cavaramacho's question, he asked in his turn, "And what is your favorite game?"

"The most dangerous, which puts my agility, strength, and courage to the test: I hunt the puma."

And affecting a disdainful indifference, turning away from the jaguar, he resumed his pacing with long slow strides, without even looking at the object of his greatest and inmost fears.

The jaguar raised his triangular, slender ears at the mention of his one adversary in the forest, and asked, "And how do you hunt him?"

"Very simply: I lead him on and then await his attack. When he springs on me, I stand firm and pierce his heart with both horns. To do that, one needs legs and sharp horns like mine."

"Deer have them, too."

"Ah, my friend! You do not realize that they lack my courage."

And brusquely, seeing that the storm had abated, he played his last card. Approaching the jaguar, he proposed, "Why don't we go out to hunt! I'll take the left-hand path and you the right-hand, and we'll meet at the bottom of the valley. There we'll join forces and see who has had the best kill."

The sly jaguar, intending to make the goat his prey as soon as he had left the cave, replied, "No, my friend. I prefer to wait for you and benefit by the fruits of your skill. You can go out alone."

And the goat, summoning the remnants of his ebbing and feigned courage, walked slowly out of the cave, expecting at every step the leap and the blow that would put an end to his unfortunate existence.

But hardly had he left the lair of the terrible butcher, when he saw, with no little surprise (from which he recovered instantly) the body of a puma stretched out, probably killed by lightning. Immediately Cavaramacho began to leap about and butt the lifeless body of the beast until Yaguarete appeared and looked at him with deep amazement.

"Did you kill him here?" the cat asked.

"And where else would I have killed him? Hardly had I come out when I realized he was going to surprise us and I put him out of the way without any fuss. Here he is now. And assuming a very arrogant posture, he added, "I offer you my company, if you are at all afraid, and we can continue this hunt that we have so auspiciously begun. We can go together along this path leading to the top of the hill."

"All right," agreed Yagaurete dubiously, "but we'll do as you first suggested: I'll take this downhill path and you that other one and we'll meet in the valley."

And without saying anything more, he started out at a slow trot.

The goat and the jaguar never met again.

Leopard-like but with black spots centering his rosette markings, the New World jaguar once ranged as far north as Arkansas.

St. Francis and the Birds

Europe (From The Little Flowers of St. Francis of Assisi, 14th century)

It befell on a day that a certain young man had caught many turtledoves; and as he was carrying them for sale, Saint Francis, who had ever a tender pity for gentle creatures, met him, and looking on those turtledoves with pitying eyes, said to the youth: "I pray thee give them me, that birds so gentle, unto which the Scripture likeneth chaste and humble and faithful souls, may not fall into the hands of cruel men that would kill them." Forthwith, inspired of God, he gave them all to Saint Francis; and he, receiving them into his bosom, began to speak tenderly unto them: "O my sisters, simple-minded turtledoves, innocent and chaste, why have you let yourselves be caught? Now would I fain deliver you from death and make you nests, that ye may be fruitful and multiply, according to the commandments of your Creator." And Saint Francis went and made nests for them all: and they, abiding therein, began to lay their eggs and hatch them before the eyes of the brothers: and so tame were they, they dwelt with Saint Francis and all the other brothers as though they had been fowls that had always fed from their hands, and never did they go away until Saint Francis with his blessing gave them leave to go.

And as with great fervor he was going on the way, he lifted up his eyes and beheld some trees hard by the road whereon sat a great company of birds well nigh without number; whereat Saint Francis marveled, and said to his companions: "Ye shall wait for me here upon the way and I will go to preach unto my little sisters, the birds." And he went unto the field and began to preach unto the birds that were upon the ground; and immediately those that were on the trees flew down to him, and

Birds are perhaps the easiest to love of all God's creatures.

they all of them remained still and quiet together, until Saint Francis made an end of his preaching: and not even then did they depart, until he had given them his blessing. And according to what Brother Masseo afterwards related unto Brother Jacques da Massa, Saint Francis went among them touching them with his cloak, howbeit none moved from out his place. The sermon that Saint Francis preached unto them was after this fashion: "My little sisters, the birds, much bounden ye are to God, your Creator, and always in every place ought ye to praise Him, for that He hath given you liberty to fly about everywhere, and hath also given you double and triple raiment; moreover He preserved your seed in the ark of Noah, that your race might not perish out of the world; still more are ye beholden to Him for the element of the air which He hath appointed for you; beyond all this, ye sow not, neither do ye reap; and God feedeth you, and giveth you the streams and fountains for your drink; the mountains and the valleys for your refuge and the high trees whereon to make your nests; and because ye know not how to spin or sew, God clotheth you, you and your children; wherefore your Creator loveth you much, seeing He hath bestowed on you so many benefits; and therefore, my little sisters, beware of the sin of ingratitude, and study always to give praises unto God." Whenas Saint Francis spake these words to them, those birds began all of them to open their beaks, and stretch their necks, and spread their wings, and reverently bend their heads down to the ground, and by their acts and by their songs to show that the holy Father gave them joy exceeding great. And Saint Francis rejoiced with them, and was glad, and

Do birds sing because St. Francis bade them? There was a real St. Francis, born Giovanni di Bernardone in 1181. He gave away his wealth and roamed Europe, preaching peace and humility as well as love and respect for all living creatures.

marveled much at so great a company of birds and their most beautiful diversity and their good heed and sweet friendliness, for which cause he devoutly praised their Creator in them. At the last, having ended the preaching, Saint Francis made over them the sign of the cross, and gave them leave to go away; and thereby with wondrous singing all the birds rose up in the air; and then, in the fashion of the cross that Saint Francis had made over them, divided themselves into four parts; and the one part flew toward the East, and the other toward the West, and the other toward the South, and the fourth toward the North, and each flight went on its way singing wondrous songs.

ANIMAL MAGIC

In the ancient world there was no rigid dividing line between the natural and the supernatural. It seemed quite possible that animals could turn into men or men into animals; that gods or demons might take the shape of beasts or birds. Primitive man believed that what he did could influence animals—as when he performed magic rites to ensure a successful hunt—and he also believed that animals' lives influenced his. Remnants of this belief linger for those of us who feel uneasy when a black cat crosses our path.

There is probably no living creature who has not been, at one time or another, the subject of a superstitious belief. Most often, but not always, white animals symbolize good, and black, evil.

Cats have, over the centuries, been credited with more than their share of supernatural significance.

Cats are welcomed into Mohammedan mosques as symbols of good luck. The prophet Mohammed was himself fond of cats and when, one day, a cat was asleep on the sleeve of his coat, he cut off the sleeve rather than disturb her. When he returned the cat bowed low to him showing respect and love. Mohammed stroked the cat three times, conferring on her and her descendants forever the ability to land safely on all four feet when dropped from any height.

In Europe of the Dark Ages, the cat was feared as a possible witch or demon, a role the cat still plays on Halloween. It is possible that the Church helped bring on the plague by urging the eradication of cats. This caused the number of rats to increase, and it was the rats' fleas that spread the disease.

In relatively recent times the black cat has remained for Europeans and Americans a sign of impending evil, but it has been for Englishmen a sign of good luck. Some believed that stroking the tail of a black cat could cure a stye in the eye.

Cats were never more honored than in ancient Egypt, where it was forbidden, on pain of death, to injure a cat or send it out of the country. When a cat

died, members of its human family shaved their eyebrows in token of mourning and spent large sums of money on funeral ceremonies and entombing the cat, mummified, with its favorite toys and a supply of food.

Buddha is supposed to have died because a rat, sent to get medicine for him, was eaten by hence, to the Buddhist, the cat means bad luck

No one knows the source of the belief that have nine lives, but in Thailand the cat w symbol of immortality. When a member of royal family died a cat was buried with him and a small hole was left in one corner of the tomb. When, after a day or two, the cat found the escape route and emerged, it was assumed that the dead ruler's soul emerged with him, freed to rise into Heaven.

As is appropriate for man's first servant and oldest friend among ani-

Superstitions have their origin in man's tendency to project purely human traits onto animals, calling one "good" and another "bad."

mals, the dog figures in many superstitions. Some believe that dogs can see ghosts and hear sounds beyond the power of the human ear. A dog howling at night foretells death. Dogs may, themselves, become ghosts and strive to protect their masters after death.

The Eskimos personify death as an ugly hairless dog living at the bottom of the sea. The Greeks believed a many-headed dog named Cerberus guarded the gate to the Underworld. The Aztecs sacrificed a red dog to carry the soul of a dead king across a deep stream and to announce his arrival in the Other World.

There are fewer superstitions concerning horses. Long ago, some believed that the rider of a white horse could diagnose illness and prescribe for it. In England it is considered bad luck to meet a white horse on the way to work, unless you are quick enough to make a wish before you see the horse's tail—then the wish will come true. In America, farm boys used to tell each other that a hair from a horse's mane or tail would turn into a tiny snake if dropped into water. Hairs from the dark markings on a donkey—a cross-shaped marking because a donkey had carried Christ—were supposed to bring good fortune. Sheep have generally been considered lucky animals, unless, of course, they are black sheep.

Children used to go to the stable at midnight on Christmas Eve to see if the animals knelt as before the Christ Child, newborn in Bethlehem.

Some American Indians revered the rabbit as the creator of the world. Both Aztecs and Hindus saw a rabbit, rather than a man's face, in the full moon. The origin of the belief that a rabbit's foot, carried in the pocket, brings good luck is unknown.

The toad can cause warts; he may also cure them. Killing a toad can make it rain.

Rats leaving a ship before it sails—or leaving a house—forecast disaster. Rats are sometimes a symbol of night and darkness, contrasting with the lion as a symbol of the sun, and from this relationship came ancient legends in which a rat (or mouse) manages to free a lion from captivity.

According to the Navajo Indians, a squirrel's tail tied to a baby's cradle would protect it from witchcraft.

Eskimos used to preserve parts of a seal's body after a successful hunt and tie tiny gifts—like a bone needle, a comb, or a few beads—to them. They believed that the seal's soul would report on this good treatment to other seals, and that the other seals would be willing to be killed by hunters in their turn.

Some Europeans believed that eating fish made them more intelligent, and that taking a small live fish into the mouth and then letting it escape back into a stream could cure their diseases.

Birds figure prominently in the myths and superstitions of many different peoples. Often the birds are messengers between gods and men.

A good way to catch a bird is to sprinkle salt on its tail, according to one old saying.

A swallow's nest on the house brings good luck. A swallow down the chimney means that someone in the family will die. In the Tyrol it was believed

The cat as a symbol of evil and crossed fingers to ward off bad luck—both date back to the Middle Ages.

S. N. ABBOTT

Possibly some superstitions were born as practical jokes. Who but a humorist would suggest pursuing a bird with a saltshaker?

that if a man destroyed a swallow's nest his own house would burn. In France it was believed that if a man robbed a swallow's nest his horse would go lame. Czech girls believed that if they saw the first swallow of spring singly, flying alone, they would marry within a year.

Peacocks, because of their beauty and proud bearing, were usually considered royal or sacred birds, and their feathers, patterned with eyes, brought either bad or good luck. In India travelers carried peacock feathers to protect them from snakes, and Moslems carried umbrellas made of peacock feathers over important personages to protect them from evil spirits. More recently, in America, it has been considered bad luck to bring peacock feathers into the house as decorations.

Throughout Europe there survive ancient legends having to do with people turning into swans, or swans into people. The ballet "Swan Lake" is based on one such legend; another tells of the god Zeus changing himself into a swan and making love to Leda. Some tribes considered a swan the mother of the race. In Siberia, killing a swan was supposed to bring misfortune or death.

The albatross usually meant ill luck, as in Coleridge's poem "The Rime of the Ancient Mariner," and an albatross flying around a ship in mid-ocean was supposed to be a sign of stormy weather.

Blackbirds, crows and ravens are usually signs of bad luck, probably because of their color. The

Romans believed the raven forecast death, and told how one fluttered around the head of Cicero on the morning of the day when he was killed. Ravens can mean good luck, however. Visitors to the Tower of London are always shown the resident ravens which are carefully protected from harm because it is believed that if ravens ever disappear from the Tower the royal house will fall and Britain with it.

The creature that is white in color, like the stork, comes to represent good fortune.

A stork's nest on the roof brings good fortune and protection from fire. A white stork foretells a dry year, a black stork a rainy season. When storks are seen circling a group of people, one of the people will die. As for storks bringing babies, this belief comes from Germany and is of fairly recent origin.

The owl is probably the most unlucky of all birds. The mournful cry of the owl forecasts death; Eskimos say that a person about to die will hear the owl call his name. When an owl perches on a building, someone inside is bound to die; if the owl nests on the structure, the place will be forever haunted by ghosts. Greek and Latin writers called the owl "bird of ill omen," and the Bible associates the owl with misery and dissolution. Persians called the owl "angel of death." A very few superstitions have something good to say about this nocturnal,

mournful-voiced bird: in England owls are nailed to barn doors with their wings outspread, to prevent damage from hail or lightning, and in India owl feathers are placed beneath a child's pillow to bring restful sleep.

The cock—or rooster—crows to welcome the dawn and therefore can frighten away the evil spirits of darkness. For this reason the cock's image was often placed on church steeples and weather vanes. The cock also symbolized sexual prowess, and Hungarian bridegrooms used to carry cocks to the wedding ceremony. At one time cocks were used to identify criminals. The bird would be placed under a bucket and the suspects lined up before it. Each had to touch the bucket, and the cock would crow at the touch of the guilty one.

A cock crowing at the house door forecast the arrival of strangers, and the crowing of a cock at the farm gate meant rain within 24 hours.

Butterflies have been associated with the souls of humans leaving their bodies after death. A gold butterfly at a funeral means long lives for the mourners. The person who first sees in spring a white butterfly (rather than a colored one) will have good luck all that year.

Beetles generally mean bad luck, while spiders mean good luck, especially in the house. "If you wish to live and thrive, let a spider run alive." If a spider drops onto a person from the ceiling, that person will inherit money.

Bees have often been credited with supernatural knowledge. It was once believed that a girl who was

66

a virgin could pass through a swarm of bees without being stung. In England it was for many years a custom to inform the bees of a death in the family—the person sent to tell them struck each hive three times with a key and then said aloud the name of the dead person—otherwise the bees would leave the property and never return.

The superstitions that endure longest may be those connected with animals' ability to forecast weather. When squirrels have unusually furry tails and when they gather large stocks of nuts, a hard winter is ahead. The center stripe on the brown-and-black caterpillar called the woolly bear indicates how long or short the cold winter will be in relation to the milder autumn and spring. Swallows fly low, cats sneeze, and cows lie down in the field before rain. In rural America these "signs" are still observed and discussed, and some people find them as accurate as the forecasts of television weathermen!

The creature that is dark in color is usually a symbol of bad luck. If he is of nocturnal habits—like the owl—he inspires awe, if not downright fear.

ANIMAL
STORIES THAT TEACH

Among the oldest stories known today are the tales of walking, talking animals we call fables. Typically, such stories are short, pointed and easily remembered. Most teach a moral lesson, and this lesson is often restated in one sentence at the end of the tale. All of these stories existed for centuries before they were collected and printed in books, but the remarkable thing about them is not how long they have endured but how widely they have traveled. Stories that originated in India or Egypt appeared in Greek as Aesop's Fables; *the same stories were retold in exquisite French by La Fontaine in the 1660s. Translated into English, they later appeared in "readers" that served generations of schoolchildren in England and in the United States.*

Morals alone have not made these tales immortal; rather, they have survived because they are lively and amusing and because the animals that are their heroes and villains are fascinating characters.

The Leopard Who Killed the Goats

Once a leopard cub wandered away from his home into the grasslands where the elephant herds grazed. He was too young to know his danger. While the elephants grazed, one of them stepped upon the leopard cub by accident, and killed him. Other leopards found the body of the cub soon after, and they rushed to his father to tell him of the tragedy.

"Your son is dead!" they told him. "We found him in the valley!"

The father leopard was overcome with grief.

"Ah, who has killed him? Tell me, so that I can avenge his death!"

"The elephants have killed him," they said.

"What? The elephants?" the father leopard said with surprise in his voice.

"Yes, the elephants," the leopards repeated.

He thought for a minute.

"No, it is not the elephants. It is the goats who have killed him. Yes, the goats, it is they who have done this awful thing to me!"

So the father leopard went out in a fit of terrible rage and found a herd of goats grazing in the hills, and he slaughtered many of them in revenge.

And even now, when a man is wronged by someone stronger than himself, he often avenges himself upon someone who is weaker than himself.

If Aesop really existed he was a Greek slave born around 600 B.C. Clever and politically astute, he used fables to gain his freedom, then power and wealth.

Jupiter and the Bee

A Bee made Jupiter a present of a pot of honey, which was so kindly taken that he bade her ask what she would, and it should be granted her. The Bee desired that wherever she should set her sting it might be mortal. Jupiter was loath to leave mankind at the mercy of a little spiteful insect, and was annoyed at the ill nature of her wish. He therefore said that, while for his promise sake he would give her the power to harm, she must be careful how she used her power, for where she planted her sting she would leave it, and with it lose her life.

The Converted Snake

A snake dwelt in a certain place. No one dared to pass by that way; for whoever did so was instantaneously bitten to death. Once a wise man passed by that road, and the serpent ran after the sage in order to bite him. But when the snake approached the sage he lost all his ferocity and was overpowered by gentleness. Seeing the snake, the sage said: "Well, friend, thinkest thou to bite me?" The snake was abashed and made no reply. At this the sage said: "Hearken, friend; do not injure anybody in the future." The snake bowed and nodded assent. The sage went his own way, and the snake entered his hole, and thenceforward began to live a life of innocence and purity without even attempting to harm anyone. In a few days all the neighborhood began to think that the snake had lost all his venom and was no more dangerous, and so everyone began to tease him. Some pelted him; others dragged him mercilessly by the tail, and in this way there was no end to his troubles. Fortunately the sage again passed by that way and, seeing the bruised and battered condition of the good snake, was very much moved, and inquired the cause of his distress. At this the snake replied: "Sir, this is because I do not injure anyone after your advice. But alas! they are so merciless!" The sage smilingly said: "My dear friend, I simply advised you not to bite anyone, but I did not tell you not to frighten others. Although you should not bite any creature, still you should keep everyone at a considerable distance by hissing at them."

Similarly, if thou livest in the world, make thyself feared and respected. Do not injure anyone, but be not at the same time injured by others.

The Hare and the Hound

A Dog, having given a long chase to a fine Hare, that showed himself to be a splendid runner, was at length forced, by want of breath, to give over the pursuit. The owner of the Dog thereupon taunted him upon his want of spirit in having allowed himself to be beaten by the Hare. "Ah, master," answered the Dog, "it's all very well for you to laugh, but we had not the same stake at hazard. He was running for his life, while I was only running for my dinner."

He with the longer legs is not always the winner of the race. One had better have less considerable talent and use it with more discretion.

The Field Mouse and the Town Mouse

A Field Mouse had a friend who lived in a house in town. Now the Town Mouse was asked by the Field Mouse to dine with him, and out he went and sat down to a meal of corn and wheat.

"Do you know, my friend," said he, "that you live a mere ant's life out here? Why, I have all kinds of things at home. Come, and enjoy them."

So the two set off for town, and there the Town Mouse showed his beans and meal, his dates, too, and his cheese and fruit and honey. And as the Field Mouse ate, drank, and was merry, he thought how rich his friend was, and how poor he was.

But as they ate, a man all at once came into the room, and the Mice were in such a fear that they ran into a crack, in the wall.

Then, when they would eat some nice figs, in came a maid to get a pot of honey or a bit of cheese; and when they saw her, they hid in a hole.

Then the Field Mouse would eat no more, but said to the Town Mouse, "Do as you like, my good friend; eat all you want and have your fill of good things, but you will always be in fear of your life. As for me, poor Mouse, who have only corn and wheat, I will live on at home in no fear of anyone."

The Horse and the Stag

The Horse, having quarreled with the Stag, and being unable to revenge himself upon his enemy, came to a Man and begged his help. He allowed the Man to saddle and bridle him, and together they ran down the Stag and killed him. The Horse neighed with joy, and thanking his rider warmly, asked him now to remove his saddle and let him go. "No, no," said the Man; "you are much too useful to me as you are." The Horse thenceforward served the Man, and found that he had gratified his revenge at the cost of his liberty.

If you allow men to use you for your own purposes, they will use you for theirs.

LEFT A2

The pampered pet can change into the savage preying creature of the wilds; the wise mouse flees when this monster prowls.

The Mice in Council

Once upon a time the Mice, being sadly distressed by the persecution of the Cat, resolved to call a meeting to decide upon the best means of getting rid of this continual annoyance. Many plans were discussed and rejected.

At last a young Mouse got up and proposed that a Bell should be hung round the Cat's neck, that they might for the future always have notice of her coming and so be able to escape. This proposition was hailed with the greatest applause, and was agreed to at once unanimously. Upon this, an old Mouse, who had sat silent all the while, got up and said that he considered the contrivance most ingenious, and that it would, no doubt, be quite successful; but he had only one short question to put; namely, which of them it was who would Bell the Cat?

It is one thing to propose, another to execute.

The Kid and the Wolf

A Kid, being mounted on the roof of a lofty house and seeing a Wolf pass below, began to revile him. The Wolf merely stopped to reply, "Coward! it is not you who revile me, but the place on which you are standing."

The Fox and the Grapes

A Fox, just at the time of the vintage, stole into a vineyard where the ripe sunny Grapes were trellised up on high in most tempting show. He made many a spring and a jump after the luscious prize; but, failing in all his attempts, he muttered as he retreated, "Well! what does it matter! The Grapes are sour!"

The Frogs Desiring a King

Frogs were living as happy as could be in a marshy swamp that just suited them; they went splashing about, caring for nobody and nobody troubling with them.

But some of them thought that this was not right, that they should have a king and a proper constitution, so they determined to send up a petition to Jove to give them what they wanted. "Mighty Jove," they cried, "send unto us a king that will rule over us and keep us in order." Jove laughed at their croaking, and threw down into the swamp a huge Log, which came down—kersplash—into the water. The Frogs were frightened out of their lives by the commotion made in their midst, and all rushed to the bank to look at the horrible monster; but after a time, seeing that it did not move, one or two of the boldest of them ventured out toward the Log, and even dared to touch it; still it did not move. Then the greatest hero of the Frogs jumped upon the Log and commenced dancing up and down upon it; thereupon all the Frogs came and did the same; and for some time the Frogs went about their business every day without taking the slightest notice of their new King Log lying in their midst.

But this did not suit them, so they sent another petition to Jove, and said to him: "We want a real king; one that will really rule over us." Now this made Jove angry, so he sent among them a big Stork that soon set to work gobbling them all up. Then the Frogs repented when too late.

Better no rule than cruel rule.

The Shepherd Boy

There was once a young Shepherd Boy who tended his sheep at the foot of a mountain near a dark forest. It was rather lonely for him all day, so he thought upon a plan by which he could get a little company and some excitement. He rushed down toward the village calling out "Wolf! Wolf!" and the villagers came out to meet him, and some of them stopped with him for a considerable time. This pleased the boy so much that a few days afterwards he tried the same trick, and again the villagers came to help.

But shortly after this a Wolf actually did come out from the forest, and began to worry the sheep, and the boy of course cried out "Wolf! Wolf!" still louder than before.

But this time the villagers, who had been fooled twice before, thought the boy was again deceiving them, and nobody stirred to come to his help. So the Wolf made a good meal off the boy's flock, and when the boy complained, the wise man of the village said:

A liar will not be believed, even when he speaks the truth.

The Birds, the Beasts and the Bat

Once upon a time a fierce war was waged between the Birds and the Beasts. The Bat at first fought on the side of the Birds, but later on in the day the tide of battle ran so much in favor of the Beasts that he changed over and fought on the other side. Owing mainly, however, to the admirable conduct and courage of the Eagle, the tide once more, and finally, turned in favor of the Birds. The Bat, to save his life and escape the shame of falling into the hands of his deserted friends, fled, and has ever since skulked in caves and hollow trees, coming out only in the dusk, when the Birds are gone to roost.

He that is neither one thing nor the other has no friends.

Androcles and the Lion

A slave named Androcles once escaped from his master and fled to the forest. There he came upon a Lion lying down moaning and groaning. At first he turned to flee, but finding that the Lion did not pursue him, he turned back. As he came near, the Lion put out his paw, which was all swollen and bleeding, and

Androcles found that a huge thorn had got into it. He pulled out the thorn and bound up the paw of the Lion, who was soon able to rise and lick the hand of Androcles like a dog. Then the Lion took Androcles to his cave, and every day used to bring him meat from which to

live. But shortly afterwards both Androcles and the Lion were captured, and the slave was sentenced to be thrown to the Lion, after the latter had been kept without food for several days. The Emperor and all his Court came to see the spectacle, and Androcles was led out into the middle of the arena. Soon the Lion was let loose from his den, and rushed toward his victim. But as soon as he came near to Androcles he recognized his friend, and fawned upon him, and licked his hands like a friendly dog. The Emperor, surprised at this,

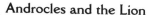

summoned Androcles to him, who told him the whole story. Whereupon the slave was pardoned and freed, and the Lion let loose to his native forest.

Gratitude is the sign of noble souls.

73

BRER RABBIT AND THE TAR-BABY
by Joel Chandler Harris

Unlike the fables of Aesop and La Fontaine, the animal stories collected by Joel Chandler Harris in the American South were intended only to amuse. The tar-baby story is an African folktale brought to North America by the first black slaves and adapted, over the years, to include names of American rather than African animals; while other Uncle Remus stories contain elements from Ameri-

can Indian, European and even South American folklore. Uncle Remus is Harris' own creation, but he is based on elderly storytellers Harris knew as a boy before the Civil War. Harris, whose sharp ear for dialect gives the stories their special charm, was an Atlanta newspaperman who wrote numerous poems, articles and editorials for The Saturday Evening Post between 1900 and 1908.

Uncle Remus as he appeared in the Post *in 1904.*

One evening recently, the lady whom Uncle Remus calls "Miss Sally" missed her little seven-year-old boy. Making a search for him through the house and through the yard, she heard the sound of voices in the old man's cabin, and, looking through the window, saw the child sitting by Uncle Remus. His head rested against the old man's arm, and he was gazing with an expression of the most intense interest into the rough, weather-beaten face that beamed so kindly upon him. This is what "Miss Sally" heard:

"Bimeby, one day, arter Brer Fox bin doin' all dat he could fer ter ketch Brer Rabbit, en Brer Rabbit bin doin' all he could fer to keep 'im fum it, Brer Fox say to hisse'f dat he'd put up a game on Brer Rabbit, en he ain't mo'n got de wuds out'n his mouf twel Brer Rabbit come a lopin' up de big road, lookin' des ez plump, en ez fat, en ez sassy ez a Moggin hoss in a barley-patch.

" 'Hol' on dar, Brer Rabbit,' sez Brer Fox, sezee.

" 'I ain't got time, Brer Fox,' sez Brer Rabbit, sezee, sorter mendin' his licks.

" 'I wanter have some confab wid you, Brer Rabbit,' sez Brer Fox, sezee.

" 'All right, Brer Fox, but you better holler fum whar you stan'. I'm monstus full er fleas dis mawnin',' sez Brer Rabbit, sezee.

" 'I seed Brer B'ar yistiddy,' sez Brer Fox, sezee, 'en he sorter rake me over de coals kaze you en me ain't make frens en live naberly, en I told 'im dat I'd see you.'

"Den Brer Rabbit he scratch one year wid his off hinefoot sorter jub'usly, en den he ups en sez, sezee:

" 'All a settin', Brer Fox. Spose'n you drap roun' ter-morrer en take dinner wid me. We ain't got no great doin's at our house, but I speck de old 'oman en de chilluns kin scramble roun' en git up sump'n fer ter stay yo' stummuck.'

" 'I'm 'gree'ble, Brer Rabbit,' sez Brer Fox.

" 'Den I'll 'pen' on you,' sez Brer Rabbit, sezee.

"Nex' day, Mr. Rabbit an' Miss Rabbit got up soon, 'fo' day, en raided on a gyarden like Miss Sally's out dar, en got some cabbiges en som roas'n years, en some sparrer-grass, en dey fix up a smashin' dinner. Bimeby one er de little Rabbits, playin' out in de backyard, come runnin' in hollerin', 'Oh, ma! oh, ma! I seed Mr. Fox a comin'!' En den Brer Rabbit he tuck de chilluns by der years en make um set down, en den him and Miss Rabbit sorter dally roun' waitin' for Brer Fox. En dey keep on waitin', but no Brer Fox ain't come. Atter 'while Brer Rabbit goes to de do', easy like, en peep out, en dar, stickin' fum behime de cornder, wuz de tip-en' er Brer Fox' tail. Den Brer Rabbit shot de do' en sot

74

In folklore the fox is always clever, the rabbit gentle and a bit gullible, the bear clumsy and not very bright.

down, en put his paws behime his years en begin fer ter sing:

"'De place wharbouts you spill de grease,
   Right dar you er boun' ter slide,
  An' whar you fine a bunch er ha'r,
   You'll sholy fine de hide.'

"Nex' day, Brer Fox sont word by Mr. Mink, en skuze hisse'f kaze he wuz too sick fer ter come, en he ax Brer Rabbit fer to come en take dinner wid him, en Brer Rabbit say he wuz 'gree'ble.

"Bimeby, w'en de shadders wuz at der shortes', Brer Rabbit he sorter brush up en santer down ter Brer Fox's house, en w'en he got dar, he hear somebody groanin', en he look in de do' en dar he see Brer Fox settin' up in a rockin' cheer all wrop up wid flannil, en he look mighty weak. Brer Rabbit look all 'roun', he did, but he ain't see no dinner. De dishpan wuz settin' on de table, en close by wuz a kyarvin' knife.

" 'Look like you gwineter have chicken fer dinner, Brer Fox,' sez Brer Rabbit, sezee.

" 'Yes, Brer Rabbit, deyer nice, en fresh, en tender,' sez Brer Fox, sezee.

"Den Brer Rabbit sorter pull his mustarsh, en say: 'You ain't got no calamus root, is you, Brer Fox? I done got so now dat I can't eat no chicken 'ceppin she's seasoned up wid calamus root.' En wid dat Brer Rabbit lipt out er de do' and dodge 'mong de bushes, en sot dar watchin' fer Brer Fox; en he ain't watch long, nudder, kaze Brer Fox flung off de flannil en crope out er de house en got whar he could cloze in on Brer Rabbit, en bimeby Brer Rabbit holler out: 'Oh, Brer Fox! I'll des put you' calamus root out yer on dish yer stump. Better come git it while hit's fresh,' and wid dat Brer Rabbit gallop off home. En Brer Fox ain't never kotch 'im yit, en w'at's mo: he ain't gwineter."

"Didn't the fox *never* catch the rabbit, Uncle Remus?" asked the little boy.

"He come mighty nigh it, honey, sho's you born—Brer Fox did. One day atter Brer Rabbit fool 'im wid dat calamus root, Brer Fox went ter wuk en got 'im some tar, en mix it wid some turkentime, en fix up a contrapshyn wat he call a Tar-Baby, en he tuck dish yer Tar-Baby en he sot 'er in de big road, en den he lay off in de bushes fer to see what de news wuz gwineter be. En he didn't hatter wait long, nudder, kaze bimeby here come Brer Rabbit pacin' down de road—lippity-clippity, clippity-lippity—dez ez sassy ez a jay-bird. Brer Fox, he lay low. Brer Rabbit come prancin' 'long twel he spy de Tar-Baby, en den he fotch up on his behime legs like he wus 'stonished. De Tar-Baby, she sot dar, she did, en Brer Fox, he lay low.

" 'Mawnin'!' sez Brer Rabbit, sezee—'nice wedder dis mawnin',' sezee.

"Tar-Baby ain't sayin' nothin', en Brer Fox, he lay low.

" 'How duz yo' sym'tums seem ter segashuate?' sez Brer Rabbit, sezee.

"Brer Fox, he wink his eye slow, en lay low, en de Tar-Baby, she ain't sayin' nothin'.

" 'How you come on, den? Is you deaf?' sez Brer Rabbit. 'Kaze if you is, I kin holler louder,' sezee.

"Tar-Baby stay still, en Brer Fox, he lay low.

" 'Youer stuck up, dat's w'at you is,' says Brer Rabbit, sezee, 'en I'm gwineter kyore you, dat's w'at I'm a gwineter do,' sezee.

"Brer Fox, he sorter chuckle in his stummick, he did, but Tar-Baby ain't sayin' nothin'.

" 'I'm gwineter larn you howter talk ter 'spectubble fokes ef hit's de las' ack,' sez Brer Rabbit, sezee. 'Ef you don't take off dat hat en tell me howdy, I'm gwineter bus' you wide open,' sezee.

"Tar-Baby stay still, en Brer Fox, he lay low.

"Brer Rabbit keep on axin' 'im, en de Tar-Baby, she keep on sayin' nothin', twel present'y Brer Rabbit draw back wid his fis', he did, en blip he tuck 'er side er de head. Right dar's whar he broke his merlasses jug. His fis' stuck, en he can't pull loose. De tar hilt 'im. But Tar-Baby, she stay still, en Brer Fox, he lay low.

" 'Ef you don't lemme loose, I'll knock you agin,' sez Brer Rabbit, sezee, en wid dat he fotch 'er a wipe wid de udder han', en dat stuck. Tar-Baby, she ain't sayin' nothin', en Brer Fox, he lay low.

" 'Tu'n me loose, fo' I kick de natal stuffin' outen you,' sez Brer Rabbit, sezee, but de Tar-Baby, she ain't sayin' nothin'. She des hilt on, en den Brer Rabbit lose de use er his feet in de same way. Brer Fox, he lay low. Den Brer Rabbit squall out dat ef de Tar-Baby don't tu'n 'im looose he butt 'er cranksided. En den he butted, en his head got stuck. Den Brer Fox, he sa'ntered for', lookin' des ez innercent ez one er yo' mammy's mockin'-birds.

" 'Howdy, Brer Rabbit,' sez Brer Fox, sezee. 'You look sorter stuck up dis mawnin',' sezee, en den he rolled on de groun', en laughed en laughed twel he couldn't laugh no mo'. 'I speck you'll take dinner wid me dis time, Brer Rabbit. I done laid in some calamus root, en I ain't gwineter take no skuse,' sez Brer Fox, sezee."

Here Uncle Remus paused, and drew a two-pound yam out of the ashes.

"Did the fox eat the rabbit?" asked the little boy to whom the story had been told.

"Dat's all de fur de tale goes," replied the old man. "He mout, en den again he moutent. Some say Jedge B'ar come long en loosed 'im—some say he didn't. I hear Miss Sally callin'. You better run 'long."

76

WILDLIFE AT THE DOORSTEP

Norman Rockwell

MAKE FRIENDS OF WILD NEIGHBORS
by Paul Villiard

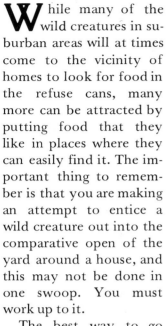

While many of the wild creatures in suburban areas will at times come to the vicinity of homes to look for food in the refuse cans, many more can be attracted by putting food that they like in places where they can easily find it. The important thing to remember is that you are making an attempt to entice a wild creature out into the comparative open of the yard around a house, and this may not be done in one swoop. You must work up to it.

The best way to go about it is to place tidbits of food at the border of your yard where the field, woods, or other shelter for animals begins. You will find that soon all the food will have disappeared during the night. This placement must be repeated each night for several nights in a row before any change is made.

Then place the food just a little closer to your house. Every three or four nights put the food closer, until finally you are putting out the banquet close enough to enable you to observe the animal taking it.

Before I go any further with this discussion, I might caution you that if you have a dog, forget the wild creatures. The smell alone of a dog is enough to keep them all far away from your place. The hullabaloo a dog usually raises when it smells an animal approaching will finish the trick.

After many nights of food offerings the animal will learn to come regularly for its handout. If you place the food out at the same time each day, you will find that the animal will come at nearly the same time to get it.

After the creature has become accustomed to finding the food each day, or each night, as the case may be, you may begin your approachment pro-

Skunks like grain, vegetables—especially sweet corn.

gram. You now do not put out the food until the animal has arrived in search of it. As soon as you see it around, put the food out, making no fast motions, and above all, not looking directly at the animal. Just slowly and casually walk out and put down the food, letting the creature see you do it.

This must continue until the animal remains while you position the food. At first, as soon as you appear this little fellow will scamper out of sight to safety. Out of your sight, that is. Rest assured you are still in the creature's line of vision.

After a bit, the creature you are attempting to observe will remain in sight while you place its food. After several days it may even approach a little closer, waiting for you to leave the food so it can come and get it. When this time arrives you have crossed the main hurdle toward making a friend out of the wild creature.

It is now only a matter of time and patience on your part until you will be able to place the dish of food right down under the nose of your furred friend of the wild! The satisfaction of doing so for the first time is a most rewarding experience to anyone at all interested in animal behavior.

Talking to an animal does a lot to alleviate its fear. You can say anything you like, since the creature will not understand a single word. Reciting the multiplication tables is just as good as speaking sentences. The important thing to remember is to talk in a soft voice, but pitched a little higher than usual, since the hearing range of almost all animals you are liable to encounter is higher than that of a human being.

It is very probably the soothing tones of a person speaking to them that quiets their fear. At any rate, it has been shown many times over that a steady, soft monologue when working with a wild creature helps immeasurably to keep it calm and relatively unafraid while in an unfamiliar situation.

If you feed animals to entice them to your land, there is one thing you

must never forget. Animals learn to depend on food put out regularly for them. Those animals and birds which normally would leave your locality seasonally for warmer climates will often remain as long as food is plentiful. In the case of birds, especially, many of the migrating species will fail to migrate if you feed them with any degree of regularity.

There is nothing wrong in this, provided you *continue* to feed them through the winter. Failure to do so will result in the death of the creatures. Many people do not realize this. At their summer homes they feed the birds daily, right up until the fall or the winter, when they close up their houses and return to their city dwellings. As they do so they are signing death warrants for all the migratory birds they have been feeding during the warm months.

The main point of this discussion is to emphasize the fact that animals act by a given set of rules. In the case of migratory birds, the combination of weather and gradual lessening of food supply triggers their migration instinct. Since cold, per se, does not bother birds too much, it follows that the main trigger must be lack of food. If, then, you supply food in practically unlimited amounts—at least regularly every day or so—it follows that the cue needed to send the birds on their way will not occur and the bird will automatically remain in the

vicinity where it has been fed through the summer.

Then you go home to the city.

Boom goes the axe! The bird would have to go back to the beginning, feeding through the summer, experiencing a gradual lessening of food supply and the onset of cold weather, in order to depart on its migration.

All of this boils down to one simple caution. Do not begin to feed any wild creature unless you are able and willing to continue that feeding right

Squirrels will enjoy helping themselves to a share of the grain and seeds you put out for wild birds.

79

Foxes generally fare well on field mice, but you can offer them chicken parts or canned dog food.

through the winter months.

Or, if you simply cannot exist without the presence of attracted wild creatures around your home, and you are there only during the summer months, then stop the feeding not later than early August, so that the animals and birds can go through the all-important triggering sequences.

Depending, of course, on the size of the land you have and on its topography, you can do much toward making it attractive to wildlife. If you have a pond on it, so much the better, because by judicious planting around the borders of the water you can create a minimarsh, or an ecosystem for waterfowl, which, you will find, will very shortly discover it and put it to good use.

A few ripe cattail heads shredded along the edge of the water in one strip will soon yield a dense thicket of tall reeds to delight such creatures as red-winged blackbirds and other reed-loving birds. Each planting area need not be large, but should be as large as you can make it commensurate with the total area of your holdings. Much can be done on an acre or two, and much more, naturally, if you have many acres of land. A few blueberry bushes planted where they can keep their "feet" wet will thrive and in a year or two afford food for a great variety of creatures, birds as well as bears.

A couple of apple trees planted well away from the house, down near water if possible, will be sure to bring hungry deer to your place. Deer are inordinately fond of apples. Seed grasses and grains can be scattered in long rows or rectangular plots, making sure that these are near cover of trees or woods rather than right out in the open. Such plantings are annual crops, and must be renewed each year. They afford nourishment for birds of all kinds, game birds as well as songbirds and waterfowl. Small animals also like grains; corn especially will bring raccoons, 'possums, skunks, and other small mammals. If you put out a dozen tomato plants you will delight the hearts of a colony of woodchucks.

These plantings should be made with the idea in mind that they are designed for the wildlife you wish to have around your place, and not for human consumption. That way you will be entirely free of resentment when the animals make good use of the fruits of your labors. Your own gardens should be protected from the invasion of wild things.

If you are not just living in a rural area but are actually farming a sizable acreage of land, then the attraction of wildlife can be accomplished in an easier way than planting for them. You simply leave strips of crops unharvested around the boundaries of your farm, especially those bordering on wooded areas. Cover for wild creatures is most important. They are reluctant, and with good reason, to come out into unprotected fields. Millet and sorghum grains are invaluable as plantings for game animals and birds.

On banks and runs where there is a chance of water and rain washing away the soil, the sowing of either crown vetch or bird's-foot trefoil will do much to bind the soil and prevent erosion, as well as furnish food for many birds and animals.

Seedling hemlocks planted close together in rows will grow fast to form perfect sites, as well as any deer that covers and nesting winter browse for live in the area.

For deer, put out a salt block, grain, or alfalfa hay.

BECOME A BIRD WATCHER

In any popularity contest of different kinds of wild animals the birds would win, hands (wings) down.

For some people, birds symbolize a glorious freedom that we earthbound, flightless mammals can never share. Other bird lovers are attracted by the beauty of birds' songs or birds' plumage. Methodical, list-minded people love birds simply because there are so many different kinds to be learned, observed and counted. Also, of course, birds are the wild creatures most accessible to us. Birds are to be found in city parks and garbage dumps as well as on farms and in forests, and they are active during the day when we are.

Bird-watching is a hobby that can be pursued alone or with friends. The gregarious birder joins the local chapter of the Audubon Society or some other bird club and is soon involved in a variety of group activities—weekly bird hikes with some knowledgeable leader, overnight campouts at wildlife sanctuaries, the various "counts," summer camps, bus trips, cruises, even conventions where birders gather and compare notes.

How to begin?

All bird-watching starts with the acquiring of a very special kind of book called a field guide. This book lists, classifies and describes the different kinds of birds found in one part of the world. Along with color pictures it includes a wealth of information concerning the various birds' habits, songs, flight patterns and so on—all very useful when one is learning to tell one bird from another.

Next, the bird-watcher acquires binoculars, because birds won't always come close enough to be looked at properly. (Tell the salesman you want the binoculars for bird-watching, and don't let him sell you his most powerful or expensive ones.)

What else? A notebook and pencil, because you are now ready to start keeping a record of the birds you see.

The following list of lists suggests some special activities birders enjoy.

Keep a life list. Almost all bird-watchers keep a continuing record of all the kinds of birds they have identified. With the name of the species they record the date and place where they first saw this kind of bird. The list grows quickly the first few years you watch birds. After you have seen all the species that are common in your area the list will grow slowly, unless you travel. The champion observer of all time may be Ludlow Griscom, who died in 1948 with more than 3,000 species on his life list. (Scientists say there are about 8,600 species of birds in the world, and that 686 species occur in North America.)

Keep a Year List. Many bird-watchers see from record each year the birds they January 1 to December 31; over a period of time these lists will show some species becoming more common and some disappearing.

Keep a Property List. Record all the different kinds of birds you see around your house and yard. This list should continue, as long as you live in the same place. When you move, start over.

Help with the Christmas Bird Count. After you become skilled at bird identification and learn special techniques for estimating numbers of birds in a flock you may be able to help with the Audubon Society's annual census. On one day between Christmas and New Year's, groups of volunteer observers spend eight hours in the field recording the names of species they see and the number of individuals of each species in a certain assigned area. The totals are later published by the Audubon Society, and provide very useful information for wildlife and conservation officials.

Go on a Big Day or Big Morning. These are sporting rather than scientific events, and they are organized by local bird clubs. Usually held in spring during the height of bird migration when there are

Barn swallows (opposite) and flamingoes. Birds are incredibly varied as to size, shape, color but all have grace, beauty.

likely to be unusual birds stopping over in the area, the Big Day is an effort by a group to see as many different kinds of birds as possible in 24 hours. The Big Morning is similar but lasts only until noon. Preliminaries always include planning a route that includes a wide variety of bird habitats, arranging transportation from place to place, and providing food to be eaten along the way. The event ends with a banquet at which the bird-watchers add up totals, hoping they have broken last year's record.

Learn bird songs. A recording of bird songs is a nice thing to own, as bird songs are distinctive and very useful in identifying species. Without a re-

cording, you can make a start at learning bird songs by memorizing the following English "translations" of common bird songs:

Tufted Titmouse: *Peter, peter, peter.*

Cardinal: *What cheer! What cheer!*

Song Sparrow: *Maids, maids, put the kettle on.*

Chickadee: *Chickadee-dee-dee DEE-dee.*

Maryland Yellowthroat: *Wichita, wichita, wichita.*

Towhee: *Drink your tea-ee-ee-ee.*

White-throated sparrow: *Old Sam PEA-body, PEA-body.*

Yellow warbler: *Sweet, sweet. I'm so sweet.*

KNOW THEM BY THEIR TRACKS

Chances are you have neighbors you've never seen. They are four-footed neighbors with fur coats, and you don't see them because they sleep during the day and come visiting at night. From time to time they will leave messages for you in dust, soft mud or fresh snow, crisscrossing cuneiform of paw and claw, with, here and there, for emphasis, the brush stroke of a trailing tail.

Mink

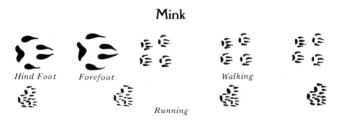

Hind Foot   Forefoot   Walking

Running

A mink groups his four paw prints close together; when he runs fast they may all be on top of one another.

Raccoon

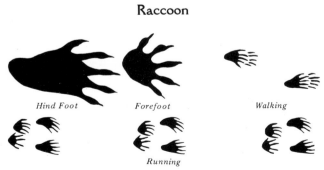

Hind Foot   Forefoot   Walking

Running

The raccoon's forefoot print is easily recognizable because of its resemblance to a tiny human hand. The hind foot generally steps in the forefoot's track when the animal is walking; when running he leaves prints grouped in fours.

Rabbit

Hind Foot   Forefoot   Walking

Running

There's no mistaking rabbit tracks. The bunny leaves four tracks grouped together with the larger hind-foot tracks in front.

Squirrel or Chipmunk

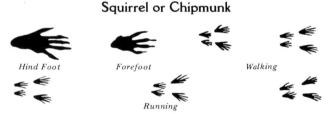

Hind Foot   Forefoot   Walking

Running

Squirrels or chipmunks leave tracks grouped in fours—like the rabbit's—but their tracks show slender "fingers" quite different from the rabbit's furry "pug."

Fox, Coyote or Wolf

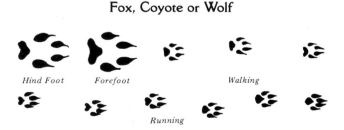

Hind Foot   Forefoot   Walking

Running

These animals leave tracks with claw marks, like dog tracks, but they place their feet more carefully. Hind feet step on tracks made by forefeet.

84

Cat

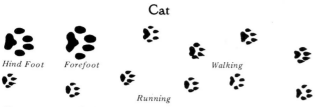

Hind Foot Forefoot Walking Running

Cats retract their claws when walking or running, so no claw marks show on their tracks. They walk daintily, placing the hind feet in the tracks made by the forefeet so only one set of paw marks can be seen. The tracks are close together if the cat is walking, farther apart if it is running. A wildcat or puma will leave tracks like the cat's but larger.

Skunk

Hind Foot Forefoot Walking Running

The skunk's hind footprint resembles a tiny human foot. The skunk runs rarely, but when he does he leaves four prints in a diagonal pattern unlike that of any other animal.

Varied and numerous are the furred creatures that co-exist with civilization in back yards, city parks, vacant lots.

CARE FOR WILD ORPHAN ANIMALS

It happens to most people, sooner or later, even those in cities. You find a cunning little big-eyed, furry or feathered baby on the ground looking helpless.

What to do?

Think twice before you pick up the darling little thing and carry it home, because playing stepmother to a wild baby requires round-the-clock effort.

The experts counsel returning the baby to its nest if at all possible—they say there's little danger of the mother rejecting the infant because of contact with human hands. And, let's face it, a mother robin or a mother squirrel knows best what's best for baby.

"Look, Mom! Look what I found!"

Return it to the nest, or leave it to shift for itself if it's able. That's what we *should* do. What we do more often, particularly if there is a child involved (Look, Mom! Look what I found! Can I keep it for a pet?) is bring the creature home and try to care for it.

Here, then, are some guidelines on when to take a baby animal into your home, and how to care for it if you do.

(1) Judge objectively the chances of the baby surviving on his own. In the case of a mammal, a baby that is fully furred, has bright, alert eyes and sense enough to try to avoid humans, is probably old enough to survive in nature. In the case of a bird, it's a matter of whether or not he can fly.

(2) If the baby is too young to survive on his own, try very hard to return him to his parents. Mother, father or both are usually in the vicinity and will show themselves if you are quiet and patient. In the case of a baby bird, look in the surrounding trees for the nest from which he fell. If the baby is warm and active, pop him back into the nest as soon as possible and go away, leaving nature to take its course. If the baby is cold and still, hold him in your cupped hands until he feels warm to the touch, and then replace him in the nest.

(3) If you are unable to locate the mother—or if

you know she is dead—the baby too young to feed himself will not be able to survive on its own. You may, if you like, take the baby home and set up a wild animal nursery.

Home Away from Home for a Wild Orphan

Once you have committed yourself to raising the orphaned baby you will immediately need to provide it with a nest and food. A shoe box should do for mammals, while something the size of a quart berry basket is best for birds. In both cases a soft piece of cloth should be used to line the inside. The bird nest should also have layers of tissue inside to ease the cleaning chores.

The nest must be placed in an area free of drafts. Additional warmth is provided by a 60-watt light bulb; a goose-neck study lamp is excellent for this task. Set your heat source over the mammal's nest so that one end is heated more than the other. That way the baby can find a spot that is comfortable for him. With the bird's nest you will have to use a thermometer to keep the temperature at a steady 95 degrees. Adjustments can be accomplished by moving the light closer and farther away or using a larger or smaller bulb.

Quick Lunch for a Hungry Baby

Now is the time to prepare some food for the baby. The basic diet for baby mammals can be egg yolks mixed with homogenized milk. Mix one egg yolk to eight ounces of milk for large species such as opossums, raccoons and foxes, and one yolk to four ounces for small species such as mice and squirrels. This should be blended thoroughly and kept refrigerated until it is needed. It will not be needed until the baby shows signs of activity such as nuzzling the cloth or crawling around. Do not try

to feed the baby before he is ready, because if he is chilled he will not be able to digest the food. When the baby appears ready, pour about ½ ounce of formula into a small clean juice glass and then place that in a bowl of warm water until the formula is warm, not hot. Feeding should be carried out with an eye dropper. Hold the baby in the palm of your hand with his head slightly elevated, gently force the dropper past his lips and slowly release a drop of liquid. This should stimulate the baby to begin licking and sucking. If your baby rejects the formula, try adding a level teaspoon of honey to the supply.

If you have taken a baby bird into your home, you can also prepare a batch of formula of about one egg yolk to six ounces of milk. In addition to this you will need a can of a complete dog food

that is as fat-free as possible. The dog food is rolled into pellets and then dipped into the formula. Holding the pellet over the bird's head should stimulate him to open his mouth, and from there you simply place the pellet in the back of his mouth. Your guest will also relish live worms and bugs from your garden, whether or not you like them.

Fortunately, small creatures mature rapidly. Whether furred or feathered, wild or of the barnyard variety, animal babies need mothering for only a week or two.

BUILD BIRD FEEDERS AND HOUSES

What can you do when the weather keeps you inside the house? Retreat to your garage or base-ment workbench and make something for the birds. Wrens and martins are in-sect-eaters, and if they take up residence, you will have fewer *mosquitoes to contend with next summer.*

by Walter E. Schutz

Three-Story 14-Family Martin House

This martin house is a familiar sight to all of us and is a perennial favorite. It is not exception-ally difficult to make since all the cuts are straight

and only a moderate amount of accurate fitting is involved. The doors covering the entrances are an unusual feature. During winter they can be closed to keep out sparrows until the martins arrive.

The entire house, with the exception of the

porches, can be made of ¾-inch weatherproof out-door plywood. Cut the sides and the ends. Nail or screw these together and mount on the ¾-inch base. Nail the porches in place from the inside.

Then make the three inside floors and the three sets of egg-crate nest dividers. Small cleats on the floors will hold the dividers in place as shown. Mount the floors and dividers inside the house. Make the doors and screw them in place. Make the roof last. It is held in place by iron angle brackets and can be easily removed for cleaning in the fall. When the doors are put in the open position, be sure to tighten the screws to keep them from shut-ting accidentally and trapping the birds.

Paint the house white on the outside only; leave the inside natural. Mount it on a pipe or 4- by 4-inch post 15 to 20 feet above the ground.

Materials

Base: 1 — ¾x14x20 inches
Sides: 2 — ¾x14x21¾ inches
Ends: 2 — ¾x12½x25¼ inches
Porches: 4 — ¾x3x14 inches
Floors, inside: 3 — ¾x12½x12½ inches
Nest dividers: 6 — ½x6x12½ inches
Divider cleats: 24 — ½x½x3 inches
Roof: 2 — ¾x12x20 inches
Doors: 14 — ¼x3¼ inches diameter

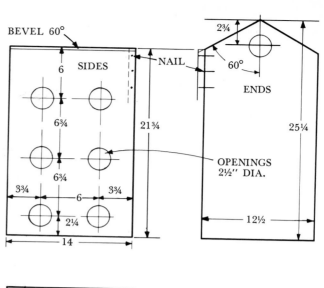

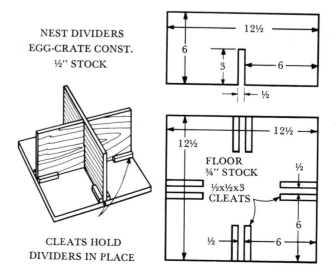

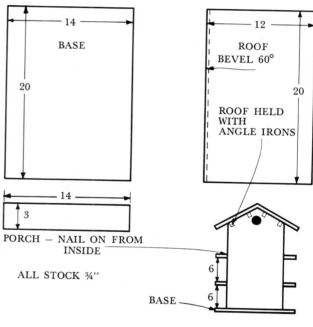

NEST DIVIDERS
EGG-CRATE CONST.
½" STOCK

CLEATS HOLD
DIVIDERS IN PLACE

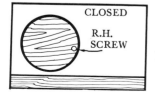

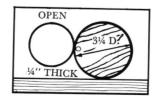

89

Suet Log Feeder

As the name implies, the suet log feeder is made of a log with the bark still adhering to it. Select any type of wood, although a hardwood such as oak is preferable. Elm makes very good log feeders because its branches are round and straight. Select a piece 4 inches in diameter, and cut it 19½ inches long. Point the ends at about 45 degrees and drill a ¾-inch hole just below the bevel at the top for the nut of the ¼-inch eye bolt. When possible use an eye bolt instead of a screw eye. Drill the vertical, ¼-inch hole for the eye bolt in the upper end.

Drill the 1¼-inch holes for the suet as indicated. These can be larger. Also drill holes for perches under two opposite rows of suet holes. Drive in the ¼-inch dowel perches.

Hang the suet log feeder on long wire away from the tree for protection against squirrels. If the feeder swings too much, attach another wire at the bottom with a weight on it. Fill the holes in the feeder with a mixture of melted suet and birdseed.

Materials
Log: 4-inch diameter x 19½ inches

Dowels for perches: 6—¼-inch diameter x 2¼ inches

Eye bolt (with nut and washer): 1—¼x2½ inches

Four-Square Wren House

The four-square wren house is simple in design and unique in appearance. The ends are 4 inches square. Drill the ¾-inch diameter entrance and the ¼-inch perch hole in one end. Cut both sidepieces 4 inches long but make one of them 3½ inches wide and the other 4 inches wide. Make the two roof boards the same dimensions and bevel them 45 degrees as indicated. Nail together the bottom edge of the sides. Next nail on the ends and then the roof.

Paint the wren house white if desired with a contrasting red or green roof. Mount by means of a screw eye.

Materials
Ends: 2 — ½x4x4 inches

Side: 1 — ½x4x4 inches

Side: 1 — ½x3½x4 inches

Roof: 2 — ½x5½x6¼ inches

Dowel for perch: 1 — ¼-inch diameter x 2 inches

Screw eye: 1 — 1 inch long

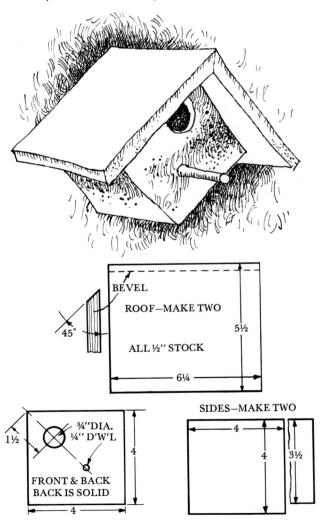

ANIMALS WHO CAME IN FROM THE COLD

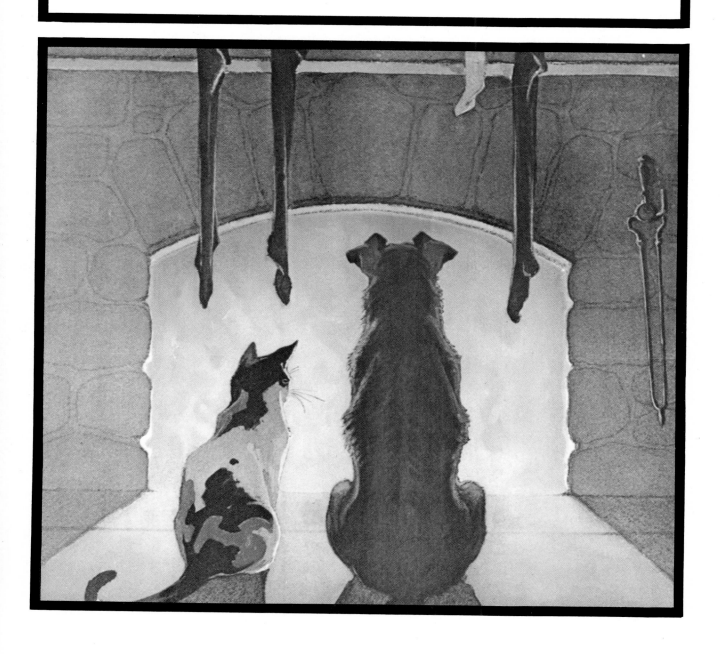

VIP'S OF THE ANIMAL WORLD—VERY IMPORTANT PETS

James Boswell wrote of his old friend Dr. Samuel Johnson in 1783: "I never shall forget the indulgence with which he treated Hodge, his cat, for whom he himself used to go out and buy oysters, lest the servants having that trouble should take a dislike to the poor creature." As it happened, this fondness for cats was one enthusiasm which the two friends could not share.

"I am unluckily one of those who have an antipathy to a cat," Boswell continued. "I am uneasy when in the room with one; and, I own, I frequently suffered a good deal from the presence of the same Hodge.

"I recollect him one day scrambling up Dr. Johnson's breast, apparently with much satisfaction, while my friend, smiling and half-whistling, rubbed down his back, and pulled him by the tail; and when I observed he was a fine cat, saying, 'Why, yes, Sir, but I have had cats whom I liked better than this'; and then, as if perceiving Hodge to be out of countenance, adding, 'but he is a very fine cat, a very fine cat indeed.' "

In this manner a cat of unknown sex and color, named Hodge, joined the select company of animal companions—the term "pets" seems inadequate—immortalized in literature. Cats and dogs predomi-nate, but the list also includes birds, reptiles, rodents and other creatures.

When he was living in London writing *Barnaby Rudge*, in 1841, Charles Dickens had two talking ravens, both named Grip, who served as inspiration for the raven in the novel.

The first Grip lived in the stable, where he preferred to sleep on horseback. He generally played the clown, but he was capable of pecking at the ankles of children and ladies, and would snatch dinner from under the nose of a friendly Newfoundland dog. One day when the stable was being painted he ate paint and white lead left by the workmen, an indiscretion that brought on his untimely end.

In Grip's last moments, laments Dickens, the bird talked to himself incoherently, then finally "walked twice or thrice along the coach-house, stopped to bark, staggered, exclaimed 'Halloa, old girl!' (his favorite expression) and died. He behaved throughout with decent fortitude, equanimity and self-possession, which cannot be too much admired." Grip I was stuffed, mounted in a glass case and kept in Dickens' study.

Grip II, who had belonged to the landlord of a village pub, soon joined the Dickens household and occupied himself with digging up the cheese and halfpence his predecessor had buried in the garden—with "immense labor and research," says Dickens. Later he began burying his own treasure: a brush, a large hammer and several raw potatoes. Housed in the stable, he picked up colorful coachman lingo. According to Dickens, he "would perch outside my window and drive imaginary horses with great skill, all day. He had not the least respect for me, I am sorry to say, or for anybody but the cook, to whom he was attached." After several years Grip II met the same fate as Grip I, though there was added this time to the fatal dose of paint, for variety, a little putty.

Gone, but not forgotten! In America Edgar Allan Poe wrote a review of Dickens' *Barnaby Rudge* for *The Saturday Evening Post*. A few years later Poe tried his hand at writing a poem about a mysterious talking bird, originally a parrot. The words began falling into place only when Poe remembered the raven named Grip in *Barnaby Rudge*, a gloomy bird who in Newgate Prison intoned portentous one-liners like "Nobody" and "Never!" Without question, Poe's "The Raven" is the literary descendant of Dickens' mischievous flesh-and-blood pets.

Three tame hares named Bess, Puss and Tiny were the cherished pets of 18th-century English poet William Cowper. Bess was the boldest of the three, in contrast to the timid and affectionate Puss, who would tug at Cowper's coat with her teeth when she wanted to go out. Considered surly, Tiny "gamboled with an expression of dignified disgust on his whiskered features."

The poet himself built hutches for the hares, fed them, shook out their straw bedding and shut them safely inside at night (they had the run of the garden during the daytime).

One summer evening the serenity of the household was disturbed when someone discovered that Puss had gnawed her way through a lattice and escaped. As Cowper tells it:

"I hastened to the kitchen, where I saw the redoubtable Thomas Freeman, who told me that, having seen her just after she dropped into the street, he attempted to cover her with his hat, but she screamed out and leaped directly over his head. I then desired him to pursue as fast as possible, and added Richard Coleman to the chase, as being nimbler, and carrying less weight than Thomas."

Returning less than an hour later, Coleman related how he had finally caught up with the hare and chased it through the town to a tanyard, where there were pits filled with water. Into the first of these plunged Puss, and while struggling from one pit into another, after almost drowning, she was rescued by one of the men assisting in t[h]e who grasped her by the ears. Safely depo[sited in a] sack, she was carried home at ten o'clock.

"This frolic cost us four shillings," wrote a friend, "but . . . we did not grudge a [farth]ing of it. The poor creature received only a little hurt in one of her claws, and in one of her ears, and is now almost as well as ever."

Perhaps the best known of all literary pets was the golden-brown cocker spaniel named Flush who lived with poetess Elizabeth Barrett on Wimpole Street, London.

"Flushie is my friend—my companion—and loves me better than he loves the sunshine without," Miss Barrett wrote. Shy and a semi-invalid, she seldom left the back bedroom of her father's house, and Flush was generally content to lie at the foot of her sofa. Maids took the dog out for an occasional airing, and on three such occasions he was stolen by dognappers and Miss Barrett had to pay ransom to get him back. Very much the pampered pet, Flush dined on roasted chicken, toast with cream cheese, and milk with a little sugar stirred into it.

Not too surprisingly, Flush suffered from jealousy when poet Robert Browning came to woo Miss Barrett—and subsequently to inspire *Sonnets from the Portuguese*. Twice Flush nipped Browning on the leg. A muzzle was considered, but true love conquers all; suitor and pet became friends. When Elizabeth stole secretly out of the house to elope with Browning she took Flush with her, whispering, "Oh Flush, if you make a sound I am lost!" Usually the dog barked noisily at the prospect of going out, but this time he kept perfectly still until they were safely away.

Flush lived out his days in sunny Italy where spaniels were a rarity and greatly admired, and where he could safely run free without a leash. "He goes out every day," Elizabeth reported, "and speaks Italian to the little dogs."

Miss Barrett wrote a sonnet about Flush, Virginia Woolf wrote a book-length biography of him, and numerous dog-actors have portrayed him in the play *The Barretts of Wimpole Street*.

The French novelist Colette wrote an entire book about her many and varied pets—lizards, grasshoppers, goldfish, snakes, a robin, a parakeet, numerous dogs and cats, and a Brazilian squirrel named Ricotte. She describes the squirrel's arrival in her home:

"The squirrel was drinking the milk put out to welcome her, holding the edge of the bowl with both hands. Then she wiped her little nose on the velvet of the armchair, combed herself with her ten fingers, like a romantic poet, scratched one ear, arranged her tail like a question-mark up her back, and cracked herself some hazelnuts. . . .

"The next day I severed her chain. How could one keep that elfin sprite, that flying spark, on a chain? . . . There she is, in front of me. The minute before she was elsewhere, and the minute after where will she be? . . . And though one of her little monkey hands is enough to cause the most artful destruction, she is extravagantly furnished with four of them!

"Yesterday the full sugar-basin upset her because she despaired of finding in the room a hiding-place for each piece of sugar. This morning she is comforted: having put the stolen pieces back in their place, one by one, she mounts guard beside the basin. I find almonds in my overboots and bits of biscuit inserted like sachets among my underclothes. There are candle-ends in my powder box and . . . and, dear me, whatever's that crackling under the carpet? Pastilles of chlorate of potassium! Ricotte's treating her throat. And we must not feel surprised if burglars get into our house in the night, because Ricotte has filled the slots of all the bolts with walnuts."

Alexandre Dumas had a special name for his collection of pets: vultures, monkeys, mackaws, cats and an English pointer named Prichard. He called them *"mes bêtes"*—my beasts. Lord Byron had at one time eight dogs, ten horses, five cats and an Egyptian crane at his home in Ravenna, Italy.

But there were lovers of pets among American authors, also.

"Papa is very fond of animals, particularly of cats," wrote 13-year-old Susy Clemens of her famous father, Mark Twain. "We had a dear little gray kitten once that he named Lazy (Papa always wore gray to match his hair and eyes) and he would carry him on his shoulder, it was a mighty pretty sight! The gray cat sound asleep against papa's gray coat and hair." (The punctuation is Susy's.)

Mark himself wrote: "A home without a cat, and a well-fed, well-petted properly revered cat, may be a perfect home, *perhaps*, but how can it prove its title?" The title of the Clemens summer home near Elmira, New York, was never in doubt as there were 11 cats in residence. Mark gave them names like Sour Mash, Zoroaster, Apollinarius, Buffalo Bill, Blatherskite, Abner, Motley, Satan, Sin, Pestilence and Famine. He explained that some of the names were selected "not in an unfriendly spirit, but merely to practice the children in large and difficult styles of pronunciation."

Mark mentioned still another of his many cats in a letter dated October 2, 1908:

"Dear Mrs. Patterson—The contents of your letter are very pleasant and very welcome, and I thank you for them, sincerely. If I can find a photograph of my Tammany and her kittens I will enclose it in this. One of them likes to be crammed into a corner-pocket of the billiard table—which he fits as snugly as does a finger in a glove—and then he watches a game (and obstructs it) by the hour, and spoils many a shot by putting out his paw and changing the direction of a passing ball. Whenever a ball is in his arms, or so close to him that it cannot be played upon without risk of hurting him, the player is privileged to remove it to any one of the three spots that chances to be vacant. . . ."

Cats figure in several of Mark Twain's stories, but the best known of his fictional felines is Dick Baker's cat in *Roughing It*. Dick Baker is a gold prospector and Tom Quartz, who ranges the Western mountains with him, is a cat with remarkably good judgment about mining grounds.

The story was a favorite of President Theodore Roosevelt's and he named a White House cat Tom Quartz. The President regularly reported on the antics of this Tom Quartz in letters that he sent to his sons at school and to other young friends, and there was always a present for Tom Quartz on the White House Christmas tree.

Kate Douglas Wiggin, late 19th-century author of children's books that have become classics, described how, when she and her sister were young, they kept pet frogs in a fenced-off section of a creek.

"We held a frog singing-school once a week. It was very troublesome, but exciting. We used to put a nice board across the pool and then catch the frogs and try to keep them in line with heads facing the same way. They never really caught the idea, and were never in a singing mood until just before bedtime, when the baby frogs were so sleepy that they kept falling from the board into the pool. They could never quite apprehend the difference between school and pool; but at the end of the summer's training we twice succeeded in getting them into line, quiet, docile, motionless, without a hint of the application of force; tact, moral suasion, and superhuman patience being the only means employed.

"It was a beautiful sight worth any amount of toil and trouble! Twenty-one frogs in line, for a minute and a

DRAWN BY
SARAH S. STILWELL WEBER

Children and pets. Artists find the combination endlessly appealing.

half, all graded nicely as to size, all in fresh green suits with white shirt-fronts. What wonder that in various sojourns in Paris I have never been able to regard a frog's leg as an appetizing delicacy, or to hear its resemblance and superiority to chicken discussed without a shudder. As soon dine upon the breast of the family kitten!"

In more recent time, a gentlemanly poodle helped his author/master write a book that became a best-seller. The author? John Steinbeck. The book? *Travels With Charley*.

"What degree of a dog is that?" a bystander would ask when Steinbeck pulled his camper off the road at a rest stop or trailer park.

"A French poodle," Steinbeck would reply, "born on the outskirts of Paris. Officially his name is Charles le Chien. But I call him Charley." Soon Steinbeck and the stranger would be deep in conversation and the writer would have material for another chapter of his book. Charley was the friendly emissary who helped Steinbeck get acquainted with the ordinary Americans out on the road.

Charley was a natural-born traveler and early on the trip established good communications with his master. To make known his wants—for food, water, going out—he would place his muzzle close to Steinbeck's ear and say "Ftt," a sound he could manage because of crooked front teeth and the uncommon shape of his lower lip. Upon occasion Steinbeck had evidence of a more subtle communication from the dog—psychic, one might call it. Charley liked to start early on the day's journey and instead of barking would sit by his master's bed and stare at him. Steinbeck insisted that such behavior invariably woke him. "I come out of a deep sleep with the feeling of being stared at."

In Yellowstone Park Charley barked ferociously at the bears—through the window of the camper. That night he wouldn't eat, his legs jerked in his sleep and he yipped. Was he chasing bears? Steinbeck wondered if he was heeding the "pre-breed

Adults and pets. Artists find them humorous.

memory" Jack London named the call of the wild.

Later Steinbeck stopped in the torrid Mojave Desert to give Charley a cold drink. Some 50 yards away he spotted two coyotes, watching. Taking his rifle he centered both animals in the field of the telescopic sight. At that moment one coyote sat down like a dog and with one hind leg scratched its shoulder. Steinbeck froze—unable to pull the trigger. Did something of the memory of when the wolf was in Charley stay his hand? He returned the rifle to its rack, and when he drove on he left two opened cans of dog food for the coyotes.

The trip was a long one; both man and dog were tired of travel by the time it ended.

Safe home again, Charley was heard to say "Ftt."

So many loving and beloved animals are remembered because of the distinguished humans who shared their lives!

There was a pet cat, name unknown, who sunned himself on a windowsill overlooking a busy street in Stockholm. Passersby stopped to admire the cat and the beautiful voice of a child within who sang to the cat. The child was Jenny Lind.

Florence Nightingale traveled with two tortoises, a cicada named Plato and a young owl named Athena. (In Prague Athena ate Plato.)

John James Audubon wrote affectionately of a sturdy and intelligent horse named Barro who may have saved his life one day in 1811. Sensing danger, the horse refused to leave a clearing in the Kentucky forest, and there man and horse were safe when an earthquake sent trees crashing all around them.

England's George V, called the Sailor King, had the pet traditionally associated with seafaring men—a parrot. Once when the King was seriously ill the bird mourned and drooped. Finally allowed into the sickroom, he hopped on the royal bed, strutting and croaking "Bless my buttons! Now all is well." Other members of the royal family, from George's grandmother Queen Victoria to his granddaughter Queen Elizabeth II, have shown extraordinary devotion to pet dogs, ponies and racehorses.

By far the best known of many pets who've lived in the White House was President Franklin D. Roosevelt's black Scottie, Fala, who traveled all over the world with his master, attending wartime strategy meetings with Winston Churchill and other world leaders. Fala was with FDR when death came, at Warm Springs, and he appeared with the family at FDR's graveside.

George Eliot has said: "Animals are such agreeable friends; they ask no questions; they pass no criticisms." This helps to explain why Very Important People need and love their animal companions, though there may be another reason.

Perhaps these animals and others like them come to understand the responsibilities that go with fame, and they put a little extra effort into becoming Very Important Pets.

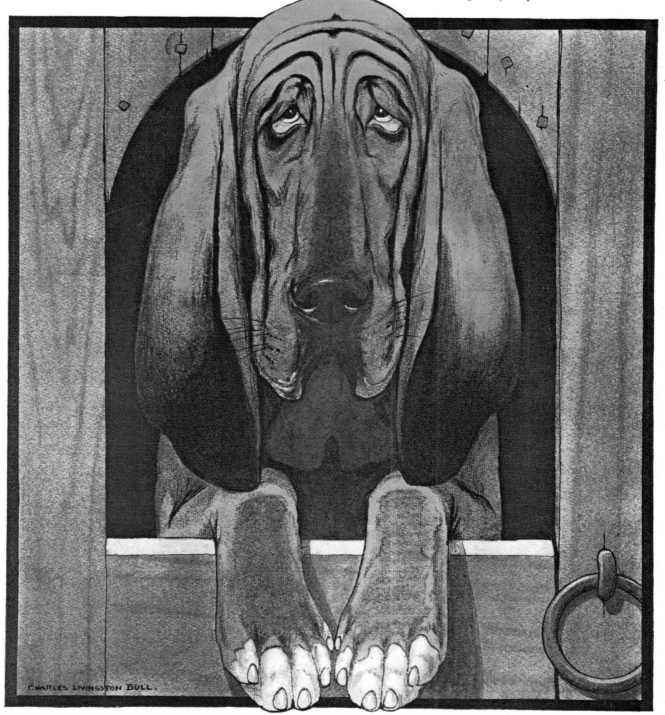

The most popular of all pets, dogs come in a variety of styles and sizes—as do the people who acquire and cherish them.

LILLIAN OF BROADWAY
by Damon Runyon

What I always say is that Wilbur Willard is nothing but a very lucky guy, because what is it but luck that has him teetering along Forty-ninth Street one cold snowy morning when Lillian is mer-owing around the sidewalk looking for her mamma?

And what is it but luck that has Wilbur Willard all mulled up to a million, what with him having been sitting out a few glasses of Scotch with a friend by the name of Haggerty in an apartment over in Fifty-ninth Street? Because if Wilbur Willard is not mulled up he will see Lillian is nothing but a little black cat, and give her plenty of room, for everybody knows that black cats are terribly bad luck, even when they are only kittens.

But being mulled up like I tell you, things look very different to Wilbur Willard, and he does not see Lillian as a little black kitten scrabbling around in the snow. He sees a beautiful leopard; because a copper by the name of O'Hara, who is walking past about then and who knows Wilbur Willard, hears him say:

"Oh, you beautiful leopard!"

The copper takes a quick peek himself, because he does not wish any leopards running around his beat, it being against the law, but all he sees, as he tells me afterwards, is this rumpot ham, Wilbur Willard, picking up a scrawny little black kitten and shoving it in his overcoat pocket, and he also hears Wilbur say:

"Your name is Lillian."

Then Wilbur teeters on up to his room on the top floor of an old fleabag in Eighth Avenue that is called the Hotel de Brussels, where he lives quite a while, because the management does not mind actors, the management of the Hotel de Brussels being very broadminded, indeed.

There is some complaint this same morning from one of Wilbur's neighbors, an old burlesque doll by the name of Minnie Madigan, who is not working since Abraham Lincoln is assassinated, because she hears Wilbur going on in his room about a beautiful leopard, and calls up the clerk to say that a hotel which allows wild animals is not respectable. But the clerk looks in on Wilbur and finds him playing with nothing but a harmless-looking little black kitten, and nothing comes of the old doll's grouse, especially as nobody ever claims the Hotel de Brussels is respectable anyway, or at least not much.

Of course when Wilbur comes out from under the ether next afternoon he can see Lillian is not a leopard, and in fact Wilbur is quite astonished to find himself in bed with a little black kitten, because it seems Lillian is sleeping on Wilbur's chest to keep warm. At first Wilbur does not believe what he sees, and puts it down to Haggerty's Scotch, but finally he is convinced, and so he puts Lillian in his pocket, and takes her over to the Hot Box night club and gives her some milk, of which it seems Lillian is very fond.

Now where Lillian comes from in the first place of course nobody knows. The chances are somebody chucks her out of a window into the snow, because people are always chucking kittens, and one thing and another, out of windows in New York. In fact, if there is one thing this town has got lots of, it is kittens, which finally grow up to be cats, and go snooping around ash cans, and mer-owing on roofs, and keeping people from sleeping well.

Personally, I have no use for cats, including kittens, because I never seen one that has any too much sense, although I know a guy by the name of Pussy McGuire who makes a first-rate living doing nothing but stealing cats, and sometimes dogs, and selling them to old dolls who like such things for company. But Pussy only steals Persian and Angora cats, which are very fine cats, and of course Lillian is no such cat as this. Lillian is nothing but a black cat, and nobody will give you a dime a dozen for black cats in this town, as they are generally regarded as very bad jinxes.

Furthermore, it comes out

in a few weeks that Wilbur Willard can just as well name her Herman, or Sidney, as not, but Wilbur sticks to Lillian, because this is the name of his partner when he is in vaude-

ville years ago. He often tells me about Lillian Withington when he is mulled up, which is more often than somewhat, for Wilbur is a great hand for drinking Scotch, or rye, or

This story from Damon Runyon's Guys and Dolls *(1930) proves that man's best friend may be a cat rather than a dog.*

bourbon, or gin, or whatever else there is around for drinking, except water. In fact, Wilbur Willard is a high-class drinking man, and it does no good telling him it is against the law to drink in this country, because it only makes him mad, and he says to the dickens with the law, only Wilbur Willard uses a much rougher word than dickens.

"She is like a beautiful leopard," Wilbur says to me about Lillian Withington. "Black-haired, and black-eyed, and all ripply, like a leopard I see in an animal act on the same bill at the Palace with us once. We are headliners then," he says, "Willard and Withington, the best singing and dancing act in the country.

"I pick her up in San Antonio, which is a spot in Texas," Wilbur says. "She is not long out of a convent, and I just lose my old partner, Mary McGee, who ups and dies on me of pneumonia down there. Lillian wishes to go on the stage, and joins out with me. A natural-born actress with a great voice. But like a leopard," Wilbur says. "Like a leopard. There is cat in her, no doubt of this, and cats and women are both ungrateful. I love Lillian Withington. I wish to marry her. But she is cold to me. She says she is not going to follow the stage all her life. She says she wishes money, and luxury, and a fine home, and of course a guy like me cannot give a doll such things.

"I wait on her hand and foot," Wilbur says. "I am her slave. There is nothing I will not do for her. Then one day she walks in on me in Boston very cool and says she is quitting me. She says she is marrying a rich guy there. Well, naturally it busts up the act and I never have the heart to look for another partner, and then I get to belting that old black bottle around, and now what am I but a cabaret performer, singing for drunks in a bar?"

Then sometimes he will bust out crying, and sometimes I will cry with him, although the way I look at it, Wilbur gets a pretty fair break, at that, in getting rid of a doll who wishes things he cannot give her. Many a guy in this town is tangled up with a doll who wishes things he cannot give her, but who keeps him tangled up just the same and busting himself trying to keep her quiet.

Wilbur makes pretty fair money as an entertainer in the Hot Box, though he spends most of it for Scotch, and he is not a bad entertainer, either.

"One thing this town has got lots of, is kittens."

I often go to the Hot Box when I am feeling blue to hear him sing "Melancholy Baby," and "Moonshine Valley," and other sad songs which break my heart. Personally, I do not see why any doll cannot love Wilbur, especially if they listen to him sing such songs as "Melancholy Baby" when he is mulled up well, because he is a tall, nice-looking guy with long eyelashes, and sleepy brown eyes, and his voice has a low moaning sound that usually goes very big with the dolls. In fact, many a doll does do some pitching to Wilbur when he is singing in the Hot Box, but somehow Wilbur never gives them a tumble, which I suppose is because he is thinking only of Lillian Withington.

Well, after he gets Lillian, the black kitten, Wilbur seems to find a new interest in life, and Lillian turns out to be right cute, and not bad-looking after Wilbur gets her fed up well. She is blacker than a yard up a chimney, with not a white spot on her, and she grows so fat that by and by Wilbur cannot carry her in his pocket anymore, so he puts a collar on her and leads her around. So Lillian becomes very well known on Broadway, what with Wilbur taking her to many places, and finally she does not even have to be led around by Willard, but follows him like a pooch. And in all the Roaring Forties there is no pooch that cares to have any truck with Lillian, for she will leap aboard them quicker than you can say scat, and scratch and bite them until they are very glad indeed to get away from her.

But of course the pooches in the Forties are mainly nothing but Chows, and Pekes, and Poms, or little woolly white poodles, which are led around by blonde dolls, and are not fit to take their own part against a smart cat. In fact, Wilbur Willard is finally not on speaking terms with any doll that owns a pooch between Times Square and Columbus Circle, and they are all hoping that both Wilbur and Lillian will go lay down and die somewhere. Furthermore, Wilbur has a couple of battles with guys who also belong to the dolls, but Wilbur is no boob in a battle if he is not mulled up too much and leg-weary.

After he is through entertaining people in the Hot Box, Wilbur generally goes around to any speakeasies which may still be open, and does a little offhand drinking on top of what he already drinks down in the Hot Box, which is plenty, and although it is considered very risky in this town to mix Hot Box liquor with any other, it never seems to bother Wilbur. Along toward daylight he takes a couple of

"Pussy McGuire steals cats, but only Persians and Angoras, which are very fine cats."

bottles of Scotch over to his room in the Hotel de Brussels and uses them for a nightcap, so by the time Wilbur Willard is ready to slide off to sleep he has plenty of liquor of one kind and another inside him, and he sleeps pretty good.

Of course nobody on Broadway blames Wilbur so very much for being such a rumpot, because they know about him loving Lillian Withington and losing her, and it is considered a reasonable excuse in this town for a guy to do some drinking when he loses a doll, which is why there is so much drinking here, but it is a mystery to one and all how Wilbur stands all this

"Lillian makes it very tough indeed on the pooches in the neighborhood of the Brussels. . ."

liquor without croaking. The cemeteries are full of guys who do a lot less drinking than Wilbur Willard, but he never even seems to feel extra tough, or if he does he keeps it to himself and does not go around saying it is the kind of liquor you get nowadays.

He costs some of the boys around Mindy's plenty of dough one winter, because he starts in doing most of his drinking after hours in Good Time Charley's speakeasy, and the boys lay a price of four to one against him lasting until spring, never figuring a guy can drink very much of Good Time Charley's liquor and keep on living. But Wilbur Willard does it just the same, so everybody says the guy is just naturally superhuman, and lets it go at that.

Sometimes Wilbur drops into Mindy's with Lillian following him on the lookout for pooches, or riding on his shoulder if the weather is bad, and the two of them will sit with us for hours chewing the rag about one thing and another. At such times Wilbur generally has a bottle on his hip and takes a shot now and then, but of course this does not come under the head of serious drinking with him. When Lillian is with Wilbur she always lies as close to him as she can get and anybody can see that she seems to be very fond of Wilbur, and that he is very fond of her, although he sometimes forgets himself and speaks of her as a beautiful leopard. But of course this is only a slip of the tongue, and anyway if Wilbur gets any pleasure out of thinking Lillian is a leopard, it is nobody's business but his own.

"I suppose she will run away from me someday," Wilbur says, running his hand over Lillian's back until her fur crackles. "Yes, although I give her plenty of liver and catnip, and one thing and another, and all my affection, she will probably give me the go-by. Cats are like women, and women are like cats. They are both very ungrateful."

"They are both generally bad luck," Big Nig, the crap shooter, says. "Especially cats, and most especially black cats."

Many other guys tell Wilbur about black cats being bad luck, and advise him to slip Lillian into the North River some night with a sinker on her, but Wilbur claims he already has all the bad luck in the world when he loses Lillian Withington, and that Lillian, the cat, cannot make it any worse, so he goes on taking extra good care of her, and Lillian goes on getting bigger and bigger until I commence thinking maybe there is some St. Bernard in her.

Finally I commence to notice something funny about Lillian. Sometimes she will be acting very loving toward Wilbur, and then again she will be very unfriendly to him, and will spit at him, and snatch at him with her claws, very hostile. It seems to me that she is all right when Wilbur is mulled up, but is as sad and fretful as he is himself when he is only a little bit mulled. And when Lillian is sad and fretful she makes it very tough indeed on the pooches in the neighborhood of the Brussels.

". . . of course this causes great indignation among the dolls who own the pooches, particularly when Lillian comes home one day carrying a Peke."

In fact, Lillian takes to pooch-hunting, sneaking off when Wilbur is getting his rest, and running pooches bowlegged, especially when she finds one that is not on a leash. A loose pooch is just naturally cherry pie for Lillian.

Well, of course this causes great indignation among the dolls who own the pooches, particularly when Lillian comes home one day carrying a Peke as big as she is herself by the scruff of the neck, and with a very excited blonde doll following her and yelling bloody murder outside Wilbur Willard's door when Lillian pops into Wilbur's room through a hole he cuts in the door for her, still lugging the Peke. But it seems that instead of being mad at Lillian and giving her a pasting for such goings on, Wilbur is somewhat pleased, because he happens to be still in a fog when Lillian arrives with the Peke, and is thinking of Lillian as a beautiful leopard.

"Why," Wilbur says, "this is devotion, indeed. My beautiful leopard goes off into the jungle and fetches me an antelope for dinner."

Now of course there is no sense whatever to this, because a Peke is certainly not anything like an antelope, but the blonde doll outside Wilbur's door hears Wilbur mumble, and gets the idea that he is going to eat her Peke for dinner and the squawk she puts up is very terrible. There is plenty of trouble around the Brussels in cooling the blonde doll's rage over Lillian snagging her Peke, and what is more the blonde doll's ever loving guy, who turns out to be a tough Ginney bootlegger by the name of Gregorio, shows up at the Hot Box the next night and wishes to put the slug on Wilbur Willard.

But Wilbur rounds him up with a few drinks and by singing "Melancholy Baby" to him, and before he leaves the Ginney gets very sentimental toward Wilbur, and Lillian, too, and wishes to give Wilbur five bucks to let Lillian grab the Peke again, if Lillian will promise not to bring it

back. It seems Gregorio does not really care for the Peke, and is only acting quarrelsome to please the blonde doll and make her think he loves her dearly.

But I can see Lillian is having different moods, and finally I ask Wilbur if he notices it.

"Yes," he says, very sad, "I do not seem to be holding her love. She is getting very fickle. A guy moves on to my floor at the Brussels the other day with a little boy, and Lillian becomes very fond of this kid at once. In fact, they are great friends. Ah, well," Wilbur says, "cats are like women. Their affection does not last."

I happen to go over to the Brussels a few days later to explain to a guy by the name of Crutchy, who lives on the same floor as Wilbur Willard, that some of our citizens do not like his face and that it may be a good idea for him to leave town, especially if he insists on bringing ale into their territory, and I see Lillian out in the hall with a youngster which I judge is the kid Wilbur is talking about. This kid is maybe three years old, and very cute, what with black hair and black eyes, and he is mauling Lillian around the hall in a way that is most surprising, for Lillian is not such a cat as will stand for much mauling around, not even from Wilbur Willard.

I am wondering how anybody comes to take such a kid to a place like the Brussels, but I figure it is some actor's kid, and that maybe there is no mamma for it. Later I am talking to Wilbur about this, and he says:

"Well, if the kid's old man is an actor, he is not working at it. He sticks close to his room all the time, and he does not allow the kid to go anywhere but in the hall, and I feel sorry for the little guy, which is why I allow Lillian to play with him."

Now it comes on a very

"So Lillian becomes very well known on Broadway, what with Wilbur taking her to many places, and finally she does not even have to be led around, but follows him."

104

"The pooches in the Forties are mainly nothing but Chows, and Pekes, and Poms, which are led around by dolls, and are not fit to take their own part against a smart cat."

cold spell, and a bunch of us are sitting in Mindy's along toward five o'clock in the morning when we hear fire engines going past. By and by in comes a guy by the name of Kansas, who is named Kansas because he comes from Kansas, and who is a gambler by trade.

"The old Brussels is on fire," Kansas says.

"She is always on fire," Big Nig says, meaning there is always hot stuff going on at the Brussels.

About this time who walks in but Wilbur Willard, and anybody can see he is just naturally floating. The chances are he comes from Good Time Charley's, and is certainly carrying plenty of pressure. I never see Wilbur Willard mulled up more. He does not have Lillian with him, but then he never takes Lillian to Good Time Charley's because Charley hates cats.

"Hey, Wilbur," Big Nig says, "your joint, the Brussels, is on fire."

"Well," Wilbur says, "I am a little firefly, and I need a light. Let us go where there is a fire."

The Brussels is only a few blocks from Mindy's and there is nothing else to do just then, so some of us walk over to Eighth Avenue with Wilbur teetering along ahead of us. The old shack is certainly roaring away when we get in sight of it, and the firemen are tossing water into it, and the coppers have the fire lines out to keep the crowd back, although there is not much of a crowd at such an hour in the morning.

"Is it not beautiful?" Wilbur Willard says, looking up at the flames. "Is it not like a fairy palace all lighted up this way?"

You see, Wilbur does not realize the place is on fire, although guys and dolls are running out of it every which way, most of them half dressed, or not dressed at all, and the firemen are getting out the life nets in case anybody wishes to hop out of the window.

"It is certainly beautiful," Wilbur Willard says, "I must get Lillian so she can see this."

And so before anybody has time to think, there is Wilbur Willard walking into the front door of the Brussels as if nothing happens. The firemen and the coppers are so astonished all they can do is holler at Wilbur, but he pays no attention whatever. Well, naturally everybody figures Wilbur is a gone gosling, but in about ten minutes he comes walking out of this same door through the fire and smoke as cool as you please, and he has Lillian in his arms.

"You know," Wilbur says, coming over to where we are standing with our eyes popping out, "I have to walk all the way up to my floor because the elevators seem to be out of commission. The service is getting terrible at this hotel. I will certainly make a strong com-

plaint to the management about it as soon as I am able to pay something on my account."

Then what happens but Lillian lets out a big mer-row, and hops out of Wilbur's arms and skips past the coppers and the firemen with her back all humped up, and the next thing anybody knows she is tearing through the front door of the old hotel and making plenty of speed.

"Well, well," Wilbur says, looking much surprised, "there goes Lillian."

And what does this daffy Wilbur Willard do but turn right around and go marching back into the Brussels again, and by this time the smoke is pouring out of the front doors so thick he is out of sight in a second.

Naturally he takes the coppers and firemen by surprise, because they are not used to guys walking in and out of fires on them. This time anybody standing around will lay you plenty of odds—two and a half and maybe three to one—that Wilbur never shows up again, because the old Brussels is now just popping with fire and smoke from the lower windows, although there does not seem to be quite so much fire in the upper story. Everybody seems to be out of the building, and even the firemen are fighting the blaze from the outside because the Brussels is so old and ramshackly that there is no sense in them risking the floors.

I mean everybody is out of the place except Wilbur Willard and Lillian, and we figure that they are getting a good frying somewhere inside, although Feet Samuels is around offering to take thirteen to five odds for a few small bets that Lillian comes out okay, because Feet claims that a cat has nine lives and that is a fair bet at the price.

Well, that's the way it was going when here comes this swell-looking doll all heated up about something and pushing and clawing her way through the crowd up to the ropes and screaming until you can hardly hear yourself think, and about that same minute everybody hears a voice going ai-lee-hi-hee-hoo, like a Swiss yodeler, which comes from up on the roof of the Brussels, and looking up there what do we see but Wilbur

Willard standing up there on the edge of the roof, high above the fire and smoke, and yodeling very loud.

Under one arm he has a big bundle of some kind, and under the other he has the little kid I see playing in the hall with Lillian. As he stands up there going ai-lee-hi-hee-hoo, the swell-dressed doll near us begins screaming louder than Wilbur is yodeling, and the firemen rush over under him with a life net.

Wilbur lets go another ai-lee-hee-hoo, and down he comes all spraddled out, with the bundle and the kid, but he hits the net sitting down and bounces up and back again for a couple of minutes before he

finally settles. In fact, Wilbur is enjoying the bouncing, and the chances are he will be bouncing yet if the firemen do not drop their hold on the net and let him fall to the ground.

Then Wilbur steps out of the net, and I can see the bundle is a rolled-up blanket with Lillian's eyes peeking out of one end. He still has the kid under the other arm with his head stuck out in front, and his legs stuck out behind, and it does not seem to me that Wilbur is handling the kid as careful

"But kittens finally grow up to be cats, and go snooping around ashcans, and mer-owing on roofs, and keeping people from sleeping well."

DRAWN BY
SARAH S. STILWELL WEBER

as he is handling Lillian. He stands there looking at the firemen with a very sneering look, and finally he says:

"Do not think you can catch me in your net unless I wish to be caught. I am a butterfly, and very hard to overtake."

Then all of a sudden the swell-dressed doll who is doing so much hollering piles on top of Wilbur and grabs the kid from him and begins hugging and kissing it.

"Wilbur," she says, "God bless you, Wilbur, for saving my baby! Oh, thank you, Wilbur, thank you! My wretched husband kidnaps and runs away with him, and it is only a few hours ago that my detectives find out where he is."

Wilbur gives the doll a funny look for about half a minute and starts to walk away, but Lillian comes wiggling out of the blanket, looking and smelling pretty much singed up, and the kid sees Lillian and begins hollering for her so Wilbur finally hands Lillian over to the kid. And not wishing to leave Lillian, Wilbur stands around

somewhat confused and the doll gets talking to him, and finally they go away together, and as they go Wilbur is carrying the kid, and the kid is carrying Lillian, and Lillian is not feeling so good from her burns.

Furthermore, Wilbur is probably more sober than he ever is in years at this hour in the morning, but before they go I get a chance to talk some to Wilbur when he is still rambling somewhat, and I make out from what he says that the first time he goes to get Lillian he finds her in his room and does not even think of him, because he does not know what room the kid is in anyway, having never noticed such a thing.

"In all the Roaring Forties there is no pooch that cares to have any truck with Lillian."

108

But the second time he goes up, Lillian is sniffing at the crack under the door of a room down the hall from Wilbur's and Wilbur says he seems to remember seeing a trickle of something like water coming out of the crack.

"And," Wilbur says, "as I am looking for a blanket for Lillian, and it will be a bother to go back to my room, I figure I will get one out of this room. I try the knob but the door is locked, so I kick it in, and walk in to find the room is full of smoke, and fire is shooting through the windows very lovely, and when I grab a blanket off the bed for Lillian, what is under the blanket but the kid?

"Well," Wilbur says, "the kid is squawking and Lillian is mer-owing, and there is so much confusion generally that it makes me nervous, so I figure we better go up on the roof and let the stink blow off us, and look at the fire from there. It seems there is a guy stretched out on the floor of the room alongside an upset table between the door and the bed. He has a bottle in one hand, and he is dead. Well, naturally there is nothing to be gained by lugging a dead guy along, so I take Lillian and the kid and go up on the roof, and we just naturally fly off like hummingbirds. Now I must get a drink," Wilbur says. "I wonder if anybody has anything on their hip?"

Well, the papers are certainly full of Wilbur and Lillian the next day, especially Lillian, and they are both great heroes.

But Wilbur cannot stand publicity very long, because he never has no time to himself for his drinking, what with the scribes and the photographers hopping on him every few minutes wishing to hear his story, and to take more pictures of him and Lillian, so one night he disappears, and Lillian disappears with him.

About a year later it comes out that he marries his old doll, Lillian Withington-Harmon, and falls into a lot of dough, and what is more he cuts out the liquor and becomes quite a useful citizen one way and another. So everybody has to admit that black cats are not always bad luck, although I say Wilbur's case is a little exception because he does not start out knowing Lillian is a black cat, but thinking she is a leopard.

I happen to run into Wilbur one day all dressed up in good clothes and jewelry, and cutting quite a swell.

"Wilbur," I says to him, "I often think how

remarkable it is the way Lillian suddenly gets such an attachment for the little kid and remembers about him being in the hotel and leads you back there a second time to the right room. If I do not see this come off with my own eyes, I will never believe a cat has brains enough to do such a thing, because I consider cats are extra dumb."

"Brains nothing," Wilbur says. "Lillian does not have brains enough to grease a gimlet. And what is more she has no more attachment for the kid than a jackrabbit. The time has come," Wilbur says, "to expose Lillian. She gets a lot of credit which is never coming to her. I will now tell you about Lillian, and nobody knows this but me.

"You see," Wilbur says, "when Lillian is a little kitten I always put a little Scotch in her milk, partly to make her good and strong, and partly because I am never no hand to drink alone, unless there is nobody with me. Well, at first Lillian does not care so much for this Scotch in her milk, but finally she takes a liking to it, and I keep making her toddy stronger until in the end she will lap up a good big snort without any milk for a chaser, and yell for more. In fact, I suddenly realize that Lillian becomes a rumpot, just like I am in those days, and simply must have her grog, and it is when she is good and rummed up that Lillian goes off snatching Pekes, and acting tough generally.

"Now," Wilbur says, "the time of the fire is about the time I get home every morning and give Lillian her Schnapps. But when I go into the hotel and get her the first time I forget to Scotch her up, and the reason she runs back into the hotel is because she is looking for her shot. And the reason she is sniffing at the kid's door is not because the kid is in there but because the trickle that is coming through the crack under the door is nothing but Scotch running out of the bottle in the dead guy's hand. I never mention this before because I figure it may be a knock to a dead guy's memory," Wilbur says. "Drinking is certainly a disgusting thing, especially secret drinking."

"How is Lillian getting along these days?" I ask.

"I am greatly disappointed in Lillian," he says. "She refuses to reform when I do and the last I hear of her she takes up with Gregorio, the Ginney bootlegger, who keeps her well Scotched up so she will lead his blonde doll's Peke a dog's life."

109

EM'LY
by
Owen
Wister

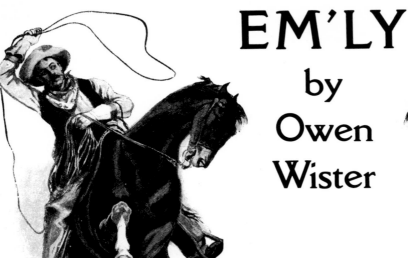

DRAWN BY
GEORGE GIBBS

My personage was a hen, and she lived at the Sunk Creek Ranch.

Judge Henry's ranch was notable for several luxuries. He had milk, for example. In those days his brother ranchmen had thousands of cattle very often, but not a drop of milk, save the condensed variety. Therefore they had no butter. The Judge had plenty. Next rarest to butter and milk in the cattle country were eggs. But my host had chickens. Whether this was because he had followed cock-fighting in his early days, or whether it was due to Mrs. Henry, I cannot say. I only know that when I took a meal elsewhere, I was likely to find nothing but the eternal "sowbelly," beans and coffee; while at Sunk Creek the omelet and the custard were frequent. The passing traveler was glad to tie his horse to the fence here, and sit down to the Judge's table. For its fame was as wide as Wyoming. It was an oasis in the Territory's desolate bill-of-fare.

The long fences of Judge Henry's home ranch began upon Sunk Creek soon after that stream emerged from its cañon through the Bow Leg. It was a place always well cared for by the owner, even in the days of his bachelorhood. The placid regiments of cattle lay in the cool of the cottonwoods by the water, or slowly moved among the sagebrush, feeding upon the grass that in those forever departed years was plentiful and tall. The

steers came fat off his unenclosed range and fattened still more in his large pasture; while his small pasture, a field some eight miles square, was for several seasons given to the Judge's horses, and over this ample space there played and prospered the good colts which he raised from Paladin, his imported stallion. After he married, I have been assured that his wife's influence became visible in and about the house at once. Shade trees were planted, flowers attempted, and to the chickens was added the much more troublesome turkey. I, the visitor, was pressed into service when I arrived, green from the East. I took hold of the farmyard and began building a better chicken house, while the Judge was off creating meadow land in his gray and yellow wilderness. When any cowboy was unoccupied, he would lounge over to my neighborhood, and silently regard my carpentering.

These cowpunchers bore names of various denominations. There was Honey Wiggin; there was Nebrasky, and Dollar Bill, and Chalkeye. And they came from farms and cities, from Maine and from California. But the romance of American adventure had drawn them all alike to this great playground of young men, and in their courage, their generosity, and their amusement at me they bore a close resemblance to each other. Each one would silently observe my achievements with the hammer and the chisel. Then he would retire to the bunkhouse, and presently I would overhear laughter. But this was only in the morning. In the afternoon on many days of the summer which I spent at the Sunk Creek Ranch I would go shooting, or ride up toward the entrance of the cañon and watch the men working on the irrigation ditches. Pleasant systems of water running in channels were being led through the soil, and there was a sound of rippling here and there among the yellow grain; the green thick alfalfa grass waved almost, it seemed, of its own accord, for the wind never blew; and when at evening the sun lay against the plain, the rift of the cañon was filled with a violet light, and the Bow Leg Mountains became transfigured with hues of floating and unimaginable color. The sun shone in a sky where never a cloud came, and noon was not too warm nor the dark too cool. And so for two months I went through these pleasant uneventful days, improving the chickens, an object of mirth, living in the open air, and basking in the perfection of content.

I was justly styled a tenderfoot. Mrs. Henry had in the beginning endeavored to shield me from this humiliation; but when she found that I was inveterate in laying my inexperience of Western matters bare to all the world, begging to be enlightened upon rattlesnakes, prairie dogs, owls, blue and

"Em'ly" is an excerpt from The Virginian, *a 1902 novel that established a new genre—the Western.*

willow grouse, sage hens, how to rope a horse or tighten the front cinch of my saddle, and that my spirit soared into enthusiasm at the mere sight of so ordinary an animal as a white-tailed deer, she let me rush about with my firearms, and made no further effort to stave off the ridicule that my blunders perpetually earned from the ranch hands, her own humorous husband, and any chance visitor who stopped for a meal or stayed the night.

I was not called by my name after the first feeble etiquette due to a stranger in his first few hours had died away. I was known simply as "the tenderfoot." I was introduced to the neighborhood (a circle of eighty miles) as "the tenderfoot." It was thus that Balaam, the maltreater of horses, learned to address me when he came a two days' journey to pay a visit. And it was this name and my notorious helplessness that bid fair to end what relations I had with the Virginian. For when Judge Henry ascertained that nothing could prevent me from losing myself, that it was not uncommon for me to saunter out after breakfast with a gun and in thirty minutes cease to know north from south, he arranged for my protection. He detailed an escort for me; and the escort was once more the trustworthy man! The poor Virginian was taken from his work and his comrades and set to playing nurse for me. And for a while this humiliation ate into his untamed soul. It was his lugubrious lot to accompany me in my rambles, preside over my blunders, and save me from calamitously passing into the next world. He bore it in courteous silence, except when speaking was necessary. He would show me the lower ford, which I could never find for myself, generally mistaking a quicksand for it. He would tie my horse properly. He would recommend me not to shoot my rifle at a white-tailed deer in the particular moment that the outfit wagon was passing behind the animal on the further side of the brush. There was seldom a day that he was not obliged to hasten and save me from sudden death or from ridicule, which is worse. Yet never once did he lose his patience, and his gentle, slow voice, and apparently lazy manner remained the same, whether we were sitting at lunch together or up in the mountains during a hunt, or whether he was bringing me back

my horse, which had run away because I had again forgotten to throw the reins over his head and let them trail.

"He'll always stand if yu' do that," the Virginian would say. "See how my hawss stays right quiet yondeh."

After such admonition he would say no more to me. But this tame nursery business was assuredly gall to him. For though utterly a man in countenance and in self-possession and incapacity to be put at a loss, he was still boyishly proud of his wild calling, and wore his leathern chaps and jingled his spurs with obvious pleasure. His tiger limb and his beauty were rich with unabated youth; and that force which lurked beneath his surface must have curbed his intolerance of me in spite of what I knew must be his opinion of me, the tenderfoot, my liking for him grew, and I found his silent company more and more agreeable. That he had spells of talking, I had already learned at Medicine Bow. But his present taciturnity might almost have effaced this impression, had I not happened to pass by the bunkhouse one evening after dark, when Honey Wiggin and the rest of the cowboys were gathered inside it.

That afternoon the Virginian and I had gone duck shooting. We had found several in a beaver dam, and I had killed two as they sat close together; but they floated against the breastwork of sticks out in the water some four feet deep, where the escaping current might carry them down the stream. The Judge's red setter had not accompanied us, because she was expecting a family.

"We don't want her along anyways," the cowpuncher had explained to me. "She runs around mighty irresponsible, and she'll stand a prairie dog 'bout as often as she'll stand a bird. She's a triflin' animal."

My anxiety to own the ducks caused me to pitch into the water with all my clothes on, and subsequently crawl out a slippery, triumphant, weltering heap. The Virginian's serious eyes had rested upon this spectacle of mud; but he expressed nothing, as usual.

"They ain't overly good eatin'," he observed, tying the birds to his saddle. "They're divers."

"Divers!" I exclaimed. "Why didn't they dive?"

"I reckon they was young ones and hadn't experience."

"Well," I said, crestfallen, but attempting to be humorous, "I did the diving myself."

But the Virginian made no comment. He handed me my double-barreled English gun, which I was about to leave deserted on the ground behind me, and we rode home in our usual silence, the mean little white-breasted, sharp-billed divers which I had shot dangling from the horn of his saddle.

It was in the bunkhouse that he took his revenge. As I passed I heard his gentle voice silently achieving some narrative to an attentive audience, and just as I came by the open window where he sat on his bed in shirt and drawers, his back to me, I heard his concluding words, "And the hat on his haid was the one mark showed yu' he weren't a snappin'-turtle."

The anecdote met with instantaneous success, and I hurried away into the dark.

The next morning I was occupied with the chickens. Two hens were fighting to sit on some eggs that a third was daily laying, and which I did not want hatched, and for the third time I had kicked Em'ly off seven

Gary Cooper was the Virginian in an early movie.

potatoes she had rolled together and was determined to raise I know not what sort of family from. She was shrieking about the hen house as the Virginian came in to observe (I suspect) what I might be doing now that could be useful for him to mention in the bunkhouse.

He stood awhile, and at length said, "We lost our best rooster when Mrs. Henry came to live hyeh."

I paid no attention.

"He was a right elegant Dominicker," he continued.

I felt a little ruffled about the snapping turtle, and showed no interest in what he was saying, but continued my functions among the hens. This unusual silence of mine seemed to elicit unusual speech from him.

"Yu' see, that rooster he'd always lived round

hyeh when the Judge was a bachelor, and he never seen no ladies or any persons wearing female gyarments. You ain't got rheumatism seh?"

"Me? No."

"I reckoned maybe them little old divers yu' got damp goin' afteh—" He paused.

"Oh, no, not in the least, thank you."

"Yu' seemed sort o' grave this mawnin', and I'm cert'nly glad it ain't them divers."

"Well, the rooster?" I inquired finally.

"Oh, him! He weren't raised where he could see petticoats. Mrs. Henry she come hyeh from the railroad with the Judge afteh dark. Next mawnin' early she walked out to view her new home, and the rooster was a-feedin' by the door, and he seen her. Well, seh, he screeched that awful I run out of the bunkhouse; and he jus' went over the fence and took down Sunk Creek shoutin' fire, right along. He has never come back."

"There's a hen over there now that has no judgment," I said, indicating Em'ly. She had got herself outside the house, and was on the bars of a corral, her vociferations reduced to an occasional squawk. I told him about the potatoes.

"I never knowed her name before," said he. "That runaway rooster, he hated her. And she hated him same as she hates 'em all."

"I named her myself," said I, "after I came to notice her particularly. There's an old maid at home who's charitable, and belongs to the Cruelty to Animals, and she never knows whether she had better cross in front of a streetcar or wait. I named the hen after her. Does she ever lay eggs?"

The Virginian had not "troubled his haid" over the poultry.

"Well, I don't believe she knows how. I think she came near being a rooster."

"She's sure manly-lookin'," said the Virginian. We had walked toward the corral, and he was now scrutinizing Em'ly with interest.

She was an egregious fowl. She was huge and

gaunt, with great yellow beak, and she stood straight and alert in the manner of responsible people. There was something wrong with her tail. It slanted far to one side, one feather in it twice as long as the rest. Feathers on her breast there were none. These had been worn entirely off by her habit of sitting upon potatoes and other rough abnormal objects. And this lent to her appearance an air of being décolleté, singularly at variance with her otherwise prudish ensemble. Her eye was remarkably bright, but somehow it had an outraged expression. It was as if she went about the world perpetually scandalized over the doings that fell beneath her notice. Her legs were blue, long and remarkably stout.

"She'd ought to wear knickerbockers," murmured the Virginian. "She'd look a heap better'n some o' them college students. And she'll set on potatoes, yu' say?"

"She thinks she can hatch out anything. I've found her with onions, and last Tuesday I caught her on two balls of soap."

In the afternoon the tall cowpuncher and I rode out into the hills, hoping to get an antelope.

Artists tend to find humor, not pathos, in the poultry yard.

After an hour, during which he was completely taciturn, he said: "I reckon maybe this hyeh lonesome country ain't been healthy for Em'ly to live in. It ain't for some humans. Them old trappers in the mountains gets skewed in the haid mighty often, an' talks out loud when nobody's nigher'n a hundred miles."

"Em'ly has not been solitary," I replied. "There are forty chickens here."

"That's so," said he. "It don't explain her."

He fell silent again, riding beside me, easy and indolent in the saddle. His long figure looked so loose and inert that the swift, light spring he made to the ground seemed an impossible feat. He had seen an antelope where I saw none.

"Take a shot yourself," I urged him, as he motioned me to be quick. "You never shoot when I'm with you."

"I ain't hyeh for that," he answered. "Now you've let him get away on yu'!"

The antelope had in truth departed.

"Why," he said to my protest, "I can hit them things any day. What's your notion as to Em'ly?"

"I can't account for her," I replied.

"Well," he said musingly, and then his mind took one of those particular turns that made me love him. "Taylor ought to see her. She'd be just the schoolmarm for Bear Creek!"

"She's not much like the eating-house lady at Medicine Bow," I said.

He gave a hilarious chuckle. "No, Em'ly knows nothing o' them joys. So yu' have no notion about her? Well, I've got one. I reckon maybe she was hatched after a big thunderstorm."

"A big thunderstorm!" I exclaimed.

"Yes. Don't yu' know about them, and what they'll do to aiggs? A big case o' lightnin' and thunder will addle aiggs and keep 'em from hatchin'. And I expeck one came along, and all the other aiggs of Em'ly's set didn't hatch out, but got plumb addled, and she happened not to get addled that far, and so she just managed to make it through. But she cert'nly ain't got a strong haid."

"I fear she has not," said I.

"Mighty hon'ble intentions," he observed. "If she can't make out to lay anything, she wants to hatch somethin', and be a mother, anyways."

"I wonder what relation the law considers that a hen is to the chicken she hatched but did not lay?" I inquired.

The Virginian made no reply to this frivolous suggestion. He was gazing over the wide landscape gravely and with apparent inattention. He invariably saw game before I did, and was off his horse and crouched among the sage while I was still getting my left foot clear of the stirrup. I succeeded in killing an antelope, and we rode home with the head and hind quarters.

"No," said he. "It's sure the thunder, and not the lonesomeness. How do yu' like the lonesomeness yourself?"

I told him that I liked it.

"I could not live without it now," he said. "This has got into my system." He swept his hand out at the vast space of world. "I went back home to see my folks onced. Mother was dyin' slow, and she wanted me. I stayed a year. But them Virginia mountains could please me no more. Afteh she was gone, I told my brothers and sisters good-bye. We like each other well enough, but I reckon I'll not go back."

We found Em'ly seated upon a collection of green California peaches, which the Judge had brought from the railroad. "I don't mind her anymore," I said. "I'm sorry for her." been "I've

sorry for her right along," said the Virginian. "She does hate the roosters so." And he said that he was making a collection of every class of object which he found her treating as eggs.

But Em'ly's egg industry was terminated abruptly one morning, and her unquestioned energies diverted to a new channel. A turkey which had been sitting in the root house appeared with twelve children, and a family of bantams occurred almost simultaneously. Em'ly was importantly scratch-

The rooster never walks—he struts. His human counterpart is the male who expects all females to admire (and obey) him.

ing the soil inside Paladin's corral when the bantam tribe of newly born came by down the lane, and she caught sight of them through the bars. She crossed the corral at a run, and intercepted two of the chicks that were trailing somewhat behind their real mamma. These she undertook to appropriate, and assumed a high tone with the bantam, who was the smaller, and hence obliged to retreat with her still numerous family. I interfered, and put matters straight, but the adjustment was only temporary. In an hour I saw Em'ly immensely busy with two more bantams, leading them about and taking a care of them which I must admit seemed perfectly efficient.

And now came the first incident that made me suspect her to be demented.

She had proceeded with her changelings behind the kitchen, where one of the irrigation ditches ran under the fence from the hay field to supply the house with water. Some distance along this ditch inside the field were the twelve turkeys in the short, recently cut stubble. Again Em'ly set off instantly like a deer. She left the dismayed bantams behind her. She crossed the ditch with one jump of her stout blue legs, flew over the grass, and was at once among the turkeys, where, with an instinct of maternity as undiscriminating as it was reckless, she attempted to huddle some of them away. But this other mamma was not a bantam, and in a few moments Em'ly was entirely routed in her attempt to acquire a new variety of family.

This spectacle was witnessed by the Virginian and myself, and it overcame him. He went speechless across to the bunkhouse, by himself, and sat on his bed, while I took the abandoned bantams back to their own circle.

I have often wondered what the other fowls thought of all this. Some impression it certainly did make upon them. The notion may seem out of reason to those who have never closely attended to other animals than man; but I am convinced that any community which shares some of our instincts will share some of the resulting feelings, and that birds and beasts have conventions, the breach of which startles them. If there be anything in evolution, this would seem inevitable. At all events, the chicken house was upset during the following several days. Em'ly disturbed now the bantams and now the turkeys, and several of these latter had died, though I will not go so far as to say that this was the result of her misplaced attentions. Nevertheless, I was seriously thinking of locking her up till the broods should be a little older, when another event happened, and all was suddenly at peace.

The Judge's setter came in one morning, wagging her tail. She had had her puppies, and she now took us to where they were housed, in between the floor of a building and the hollow ground. Em'ly was seated on the whole litter.

"No," I said to the Judge. "I am not surprised. She is capable of anything."

In her new choice of offspring, this hen had at length encountered an unworthy parent. The setter was bored by her own puppies. She found the hole under the house an obscure and monotonous residence compared with the dining room and our company more stimulating and sympathetic than that of her children. A much-petted contact with our superior race had developed her dog intelligence above its natural level, and turned her into an unnatural, neglectful mother, who was constantly forgetting her nursery for worldly pleasures.

At certain periods of the day she repaired to the puppies and fed them, but came away when this perfunctory ceremony was accomplished; and she was glad enough to have a governess bring them up. She made no quarrel with Em'ly, and the two understood each other perfectly. I have never seen among animals any arrangements so civilized and so perverted. It made Em'ly perfectly happy. To see her sitting all day jealously spreading her wings over some blind puppies was sufficiently curious; but when they

became large enough to come out from under the house and toddle about in the proud hen's wake, I longed for some distinguished naturalist. I felt that our ignorance made us inappropriate spectators of such a phenomenon. Em'ly scratched and clucked, and the puppies ran to her, pawed her with their fat limp little legs, and retreated beneath her feathers in their games of hide and seek. Conceive, if you can, what confusion must have reigned in their infant minds as to who the setter was!

"I reckon they think she's the wet nurse," said the Virginian.

When the puppies grew boisterous, I perceived that Em'ly's mission was reaching its end. They were too heavy for her, and their increasing playfulness not in her line. Once or twice they knocked her over, upon which she arose and pecked them, and they retired to a safe distance, and sitting in a circle, yapped at her. I think they began to suspect that she was only a hen after all. So Em'ly resigned with an indifference which surprised me, until I remembered that if it had been chickens, she would have ceased to look after them by this time.

But here she was

again "out of a job," as the Virginian said of her. "She's raised them puppies for that triflin' setter, and now she'll be huntin' around for something else useful to do that ain't her business."

Now there were other broods of chickens to arrive in the hen house, and I did not desire any more bantam and turkey performances. So, to avoid confusion, I played a trick upon Em'ly. I went down to Sunk Creek and fetched some smooth, oval stones. She was quite satisfied with these, and passed a quiet day with them in a box. This was not fair, the Virginian asserted.

"You ain't going to jus' leave her fooled that-a-way?"

I did not see why not.

"Why, she raised them puppies all right. Ain't she showed she knows how to be a mother anyways? Em'ly ain't going to get her time took up for nothing while I'm round hyeh," said the cowpuncher.

He laid a gentle hold of Em'ly and tossed her to the ground. She, of course, rushed out among the corrals in a great state of nerves.

"I don't see what good you do by meddling," I protested.

To this he deigned no reply, but removed the unresponsive stones from the straw.

We use the term "mother hen" to describe Em'ly-like humans who are fussy, bossy, self-righteous, always eager to take charge.

117

"Why, if they ain't right warm!" he exclaimed plaintively. "The poor, deluded son-of-a-gun!" And with this unusual description of a lady, he sent the stones sailing like a line of birds. "I'm regular getting stuck on Em'ly," continued the Virginian. "Yu' needn't to laugh. Don't yu' see she's got sort o' human feelin's and desires. I always knowed hawsses was like people, and my collie, of course. It is kind of foolish, I expect, but that hen's goin' to have a real aigg di-rectly, right now, to set on." With this he removed one from beneath another hen. "We'll have Em'ly raise this hyeh," said he, "so she can put in her time profitable."

It was not accomplished at once; for Em'ly, singularly enough, would not consent to stay in the box whence she had been routed. At length we found another retreat for her, and in these new surroundings, with a new piece of work for her to do, Em'ly sat on the one egg which the Virginian had so carefully provided for her.

Thus, as in all genuine tragedies, was the stroke of Fate wrought by chance and the best intentions.

Em'ly began sitting on Friday afternoon near sundown. Early next morning my sleep was gradually dispersed by a sound unearthly and continuous. Now it dwindled, receding to a distance; again it came near, took a turn, drifted to the other side of the house, then, evidently, whatever it was, passed my door close, and I jumped upright in my bed. The high, tense strain of vibration, nearly, but not quite, a musical note, was like the threatening scream of machinery, though weaker, and I bounded out of the house in my pajamas.

There was Em'ly, disheveled, walking wildly about, her one egg miraculously hatched within ten hours. The little lonely yellow ball of down went cheeping along behind, following its mother as best it could. What, then, had happened to the established period of incubation? For an instant the thing was like a portent, and I was near joining Em'ly in her horrid surprise, when I saw how it all was. The Virginian had taken an egg from a hen which had already been sitting for three weeks.

I dressed in haste, hearing Em'ly's distracted outcry. It steadily sounded, without perceptible pause for breath, and marked her erratic journey back and forth through stables, lanes and corrals. The shrill disturbance brought all of us out to see her, and in the henhouse I discovered the new brood making its appearance punctually.

But this natural explanation could not be made to the crazed hen. She continued to scour the premises, her slant tail and its one preposterous feather waving as she aimlessly went, her stout legs stepping high with an unnatural motion, her head lifted nearly off her neck, and in her brilliant yellow eye an expression of more than outrage at this overturning of a natural law. Behind her, entirely ignored and neglected, trailed the little progeny. She never looked at it. We went about our various affairs, and all through the clear, sunny day that unending metallic scream pervaded the premises. The Virginian put out food and water for her, but she tasted nothing. I am glad to say that the little chicken did. I do not think that the hen's eyes could see, except in the way that sleepwalkers' do.

The heat went out of the air, and in the cañon the violet light began to show. Many hours had gone but Em'ly never ceased. Now she suddenly flew up in a tree and sat there with her noise still going; but it had risen lately several notes into a slim, acute level of terror, and was not like machinery anymore, nor like any sound I ever heard before or since. Below the tree stood the bewildered little chicken, cheeping, and making tiny jumps to reach its mother.

"Yes," said the Virginian, "it's comical. Even her aigg acted different from anybody else's." He paused, and looked across the wide, mellowing plain with the expression of easygoing gravity so common with him. Then he looked at Em'ly in the tree and the yellow chicken. "It ain't so damned funny," said he.

We went in to supper, and I came out to find the hen lying on the ground, dead. I took the chicken to the family in the henhouse.

No, it was not altogether funny anymore. And I did not think less of the Virginian when I came upon him surreptitiously digging a little hole in the field for her.

"I have buried some citizens here and there," said he, "that I have respected less."

TOM EDISON'S SHAGGY DOG by Kurt Vonnegut, Jr.

Two old men sat on a park bench one morning in the sunshine of Tampa, Florida—one trying doggedly to read a book he was plainly enjoying while the other, Harold K. Bullard, told him the story of his life in the full, round, head tones of a public address system. At their feet lay Bullard's Labrador retriever, who further tormented the aged listener by probing his ankles with a large, wet nose.

Bullard, who had been, before he retired, successful in many fields, enjoyed reviewing his important past. But he faced the problem that complicates the lives of cannibals—namely: that a single victim cannot be used over and over. Anyone who had passed the time of day with him and his dog refused to share a bench with them again.

So Bullard and his dog set out through the park each day in quest of new faces. They had had good luck this morning, for they had found this stranger right away, clearly a new arrival in Florida, still buttoned up tight in heavy serge, stiff collar and necktie, and with nothing better to do than read.

"Yes," said Bullard, rounding out the first hour of his lecture, "made and lost five fortunes in my time."

"So you said," said the stranger, whose name Bullard had neglected to ask. "Easy, boy. No, no, no, boy," he said to the dog, who was growing more aggressive toward his ankles.

"Oh? Already told you that, did I?" said Bullard.

"Twice."

"Two in real estate, one in scrap iron, and one in oil and one in trucking."

"So you said."

"I did? Yes, I guess I did. Two in real estate, one in scrap iron, one in oil, and one in trucking. Wouldn't take back a day of it."

Pets tend to be extensions of their owners' personalities. Do people choose for pets creatures like themselves, or do the pets acquire, through proximity, human idiosyncracies?

"No, I suppose not," said the stranger. "Pardon me, but do you suppose you could move your dog somewhere else? He keeps——"

"Him?" said Bullard, heartily. "Friendliest dog in the world. Don't need to be afraid of him."

"I'm not afraid of him. It's just that he drives me crazy, sniffing at my ankles."

"Plastic," said Bullard, chuckling.

"What?"

"Plastic. Must be something plastic on your garters. By golly, I'll bet it's those little buttons. Sure as we're sitting here, those buttons must be plastic. That dog is nuts about plastic. Don't know why that is, but he'll sniff it out and find it if there's a speck around. Must be a deficiency in his diet, though, by gosh, he eats better than I do. Once he chewed up a whole plastic humidor. Can you beat it? *That's* the business I'd go into now, by glory, if the pill rollers hadn't told me to let up, to give the old ticker a rest."

"You could tie the dog to that tree over there," said the stranger.

"I get so darn' sore at all the youngsters these days!" said Bullard. "All of 'em mooning around about no frontiers anymore. There never have been so many frontiers as there are today. You know what Horace Greeley would say today?"

"His nose is wet," said the stranger, and he pulled his ankles away, but the dog humped forward in patient pursuit. "Stop it, boy!"

"His wet nose shows he's healthy," said Bullard. " 'Go plastic, young man!' That's what Greeley'd say. 'Go atom, young man!' "

The dog had definitely located the plastic buttons on the stranger's garters and was cocking his head one way and another, thinking out ways of bringing his teeth to bear on those delicacies.

"Scat!" said the stranger.

" 'Go electronic, young man!' " said Bullard. "Don't talk to me about no opportunity anymore. Opportunity's knocking down every door in the country, trying to get in. When I was young, a man had to go out and find opportunity and drag it home by the ears. Nowadays——"

"Sorry," said the stranger, evenly. He slammed his book shut, stood and jerked his ankle away from the dog. "I've got to be on my way. So good day, sir."

He stalked across the park, found another bench, sat down with a sigh and began to read. His respiration had just returned to normal, when he felt the wet sponge of the dog's nose on his ankles again.

"Oh—it's you!" said Bullard, sitting down beside him. "He was tracking you. He was on the scent of something, and I just let him have his head. What'd I tell you about plastic?" He looked about contentedly. "Don't blame you for moving on. It was stuffy back there. No shade to speak of and not a sign of a breeze."

"Would the dog go away if I bought him a humidor?" said the stranger.

"Pretty good joke, pretty good joke," said Bullard, amiably. Suddenly he clapped the stranger on his knee. "Sa-ay, you aren't in plastics, are you? Here I've been blowing off about plastics, and for all I know that's your line."

"My line?" said the stranger crisply, laying down his book. "Sorry—I've never had a line. I've been a drifter since the age of nine, since Edison set up his

laboratory next to my home, and showed me the intelligence analyzer."

"Edison?" said Bullard. "Thomas Edison, the inventor?"

"If you want to call him that, go ahead," said the stranger.

"If I *want* to call him that?"—Bullard guffawed—"I guess I just will! Father of the light bulb and I don't know what all."

"If you want to think he invented the light bulb, go ahead. No harm in it." The stranger resumed his reading.

"Say, what is this?" said Bullard, suspiciously. "You pulling my leg? What's this about an intelligence analyzer? I never heard of that."

"Of course you haven't," said the stranger. "Mr. Edison and I promised to keep it a secret. I've never told anyone. Mr. Edison broke his promise and told Henry Ford, but Ford made him promise not to tell anybody else—for the good of humanity."

Bullard was entranced. "Uh, this intelligence analyzer," he said, "it analyzed intelligence, did it?"

"No, it was an electric butter churn," said the stranger.

"Seriously now," Bullard coaxed.

"Maybe it *would* be better to talk it over with someone," said the stranger. "It's a terrible thing to keep bottled up inside me, year in and year out. But how can I be sure that it won't go any further?"

"My word as a gentleman," Bullard assured him.

"I don't suppose I could find a stronger guarantee, could I?" said the stranger, judiciously.

"There is no stronger guarantee," said Bullard, proudly. "Cross my heart and hope to die!"

"Very well." The stranger leaned back and closed his eyes, seeming to travel backward through time. He was silent for a full minute, during which Bullard watched with respect.

"It was back in the fall of 1879," said the stranger at last, softly. "Back in the village of Menlo Park, New Jersey. I was a boy of nine. A young man we all thought was a wizard had set up a laboratory next door to my home, and there were flashes and crashes inside, and all sorts of scary goings-on. The neighborhood children were warned to keep away, and not to make any noise that would bother the wizard.

"I didn't get to know Edison right off, but his dog Sparky and I got to be steady pals. A dog a whole lot like yours, Sparky was, and we used to wrestle all over the neighborhood. Yes, sir, your dog is the image of Sparky."

"Is that so?" said Bullard, obviously flattered. "Gospel," replied the stranger. "Well, one day Sparky and I were wrestling around, and we wrestled right up to the door of Edison's laboratory. The next thing I knew, Sparky had pushed me in through the door, and bam! I was sitting on the laboratory floor, looking up at Mr. Edison himself."

"Bet he was sore," said Bullard.

"You can bet I was scared," said the stranger. "I thought I was face to face with Satan himself. Edison had wires hooked to his ears and running down to a little black box in his lap! I started to scoot, but he caught me by my collar

and made me sit down. 'Boy,' said Edison, 'it's always darkest before the dawn. I want you to remember that.' 'Yes, sir,' I said.

" 'For over a year, my boy,' Edison said to me, 'I've been trying to find a filament that will last in an incandescent lamp. Hair, string, splinters—nothing works. So while I was trying to think of something else to try, I started tinkering with another idea of mine, just letting off steam. I put this together,' he said, showing me the little black box. 'I thought maybe intelligence was just a certain kind of electricity, and so I made this intelligence analyzer here. It works! You're the first one to know about it, my boy. But I don't know why you shouldn't be. It will be your generation that will grow up in the glorious new era when people will be as easily graded as oranges.' "

"I don't believe it!" said Bullard. "May I be struck

There are fashions in pets. Scotties and wirehairs were "in" from about 1925 to 1935.

121

by lightning this very instant!" said the stranger. "And it did work, too. Edison had tried out the analyzer on the men in his shop, without telling them what he was up to. The smarter a man was, by gosh, the farther the needle on the indicator in the little black box swung to the right. I let him try it on me, and the needle just lay where it was and trembled. But dumb as I was, then is when I made my one and only contribution to the world. As I say, I haven't lifted a finger since."

"Whadja do?" said Bullard, eagerly.

"I said, 'Mr. Edison, sir, let's try it on the dog.' And I wish you could have seen the show that dog put on when I said it! Old Sparky barked and howled and scratched to get out. When he saw we meant business, that he wasn't going to get out, he made a beeline right for the intelligence analyzer and knocked it out of Edison's hands. But we cornered him, and Edison held him down while I touched the wires to his ears. And would you believe it, that needle sailed clear across the dial, way past a little red pencil marker on the dial face!"

"The dog busted it," said Bullard.

Man and dog—pals, partners down through the ages.

" 'Mr. Edison, sir,' I said, 'what's the red mark on the dial face mean?' "

" 'My boy,' said Edison, 'it means that the instrument is broken, because that red mark is me.' "

"I'll say it was broken," said Bullard.

The stranger said gravely, "But it wasn't broken. No, sir. Edison checked the whole thing, and it was in apple-pie order. When Edison told me that, it was then that Sparky, crazy to get out, gave himself away."

"How?" said Bullard, suspiciously.

"We really had him locked in, see? There were three locks on the door—a hook and eye, a bolt, and a regular knob and latch. That dog stood up, unhooked the hook, pushed the bolt back and had the knob in his teeth when Edison stopped him."

"No!" said Bullard.

"Yes!" said the stranger, his eyes shining. "And then is when Edison showed me what a great scientist he was. He was willing to face the truth, no matter how unpleasant it might be.

" 'So!' said Edison to Sparky. 'Man's best friend, huh? Dumb animal, huh?'

"That Sparky was a caution. He pretended not to hear. He scratched himself and bit fleas and went around growling at ratholes—anything to get out of looking Edison in the eye.

" 'Pretty soft, isn't it, Sparky?' said Edison. 'Let somebody else worry about getting food, building shelters and keeping warm, while you sleep in front of a fire or go chasing after the girls or raise hell with the boys. No mortgages, no politics, no war, no work, no worry. Just wag the old tail or lick a hand, and you're all taken care of.'

" 'Mr. Edison,' I said, 'do you mean to tell me that dogs are smarter than people?'

" 'Smarter?' said Edison. 'I'll tell the world! And what have I been doing for the past year? Slaving to work out a light bulb so dogs can play at night!'

" 'Look, Mr. Edison,' said Sparky, 'why not——' "

"Hold on!" roared Bullard.

"Now silence!" shouted the stranger, triumphantly. " 'Look, Mr. Edison,' said Sparky, 'why not keep quiet about this? It's been working out to everybody's satisfaction for hundreds of thousands of years. Let sleeping dogs lie. You forget all about it, destroy the intelligence analyzer, and I'll tell you what to use for a lamp filament.' "

"Hogwash!" said Bullard, his face purple.

The stranger stood. "You have my solemn word as a gentleman. That dog rewarded *me* for my silence with a stock-market tip that made me independently wealthy for the rest of my days. And the last words that Sparky ever spoke were to Thomas Edison. 'Try a piece of carbonized cotton thread,' he said. Later, he was torn to bits by a pack of dogs that had gathered outside the door, listening."

The stranger removed his garters and handed them to Bullard's dog. "A small token of esteem, sir, for an ancestor of yours who talked himself to death. Good day."

He tucked his book under his arm and walked away.

LIFE WITH THE ANIMALS

SULLIVAN THE LION CUB
by Rudyard Kipling

The fond father who preserved this memoir of life in South Africa with his young family is clearly the same whimsical storyteller who wrote the enduringly popular Just So Stories *and* The Jungle Book. *Of the three Kipling children only one, Elsie, lived to adulthood. Josephine, the eldest, died of fever at nine. John, the youngest child and only son, died in World War I, a battlefield casualty when only 17 years old.*

Now this is a really, truly tale, Best Beloved. It is indeed. I know it is because it all truthfully happened; and I saw it and heard it.

Once upon a time there was a bad, unkind mummy lion called Alice, and she lived in a cage with her husband, Induna, halfway up a mountain in Africa, behind the house I was living in. And she had two little baby lions, and she spanked one of them so hard that it died. But the Keeper man in charge of the cages pulled out the other little lion just in time, and carried him down the hill and put him in an egg box along with a brindled bulldog puppy, called Budge, to keep him warm.

Then I went to look at him, and the Keeper man said: "This baby lion is going to die. Would you like to bring up this baby lion?" and I said "Yes," and the Keeper man said: "Then I will send him to your house at once, because he is certainly going to die, and you can bring him up by hand." Then I went home very quick, and I found Both Babies (Daniel and Una, they were called) playing on the stoop, and I said: "O Babies! we are going to bring up a baby lion by hand," and Both Babies said: "Hurrah! He can sleep in our nursery, and not go away for ever." Then Both Babies' Mummy said: "What do you know about bringing up lions?" And I said: "Nothing whatever." And she said: "I thought so," and she went into the house to give orders.

Soon the Keeper man came carrying the egg box with the baby lion and Budge, the brindled bulldog pup, asleep inside, and behind him walked a man with iron bars and a roll of wire netting and some picks and shovels; and they built a den for the baby lion in the backyard, and they put the egg box inside the den, and said: "Now you can bring the lion up by hand. He is quite, quite certain to die."

Then Both Babies' Mummy came out of the house with a bottle in her hand—the kind that you feed very wee babies from—and she filled it with milk and warm water, and she screwed down the rubber top, and she said: "I am going to bring up this baby lion, and he is not going to die," and she pulled out the baby lion (his eyes were all blue and watery and he couldn't see with them), and she turned him on his little back and tilted the bottle into his little mouth, and he moved all his four paws like windmills, but he never let go of the bottle—not once—till it was quite empty and he was quite full. Then Both Babies' Mummy said: "Weigh him on the meat scales," and we weighed him on the meat scales, and he weighed four pounds three ounces; and she said: "He will be weighed once every week, and he will be fed every three hours on warm milk and water—two parts milk and one part water—and the bottle will be cleaned directly after each meal with soda and boiling water."

And I said: "What do you know about bringing up lions by hand?" And she said: "Nothing except that this lion is not going to die. *You* must find out how to bring up lions."

Lion country. The Kiplings wintered in South Africa when the daughters (here called "Daniel" and "Una") were small.

So I said: "The first thing to do is to stop Daniel and Una hugging him and dancing round him in the den, as they do now, because if they hug him too hard or step on him he will surely die."

This was 'splained to Daniel and Una; and they both said it would be a dreadful thing to kill a lion by accident, and they promised that they wouldn't do it if they could have Budge to play with.

Budge was a nice, frisky little puppy, and he would always come out of the den to frolic; but for ten days the baby lion only ate and slept. He didn't say anything; he hardly opened his eyes. We made him a bed of excelsior (that is better than straw), and we built him a real little house with a thick roof to keep off the sun, and whenever he looked at all hungry it was time for him to be fed out of the bottle. Budge tried to make him play, but he wouldn't, and when Budge chewed his ears too hard he would stretch himself all over Budge, and Budge would crawl out from under, half choked.

Then we said: "It is a very easy thing to bring up a lion"; and then visitors began to give advice.

One man said: "Young lions all die of paralysis of the hind quarters"; and another man said: "They perish of rickets which come on just as they are cutting their first teeth." Then we looked at the baby lion, and his hind legs were very weak indeed. He used to roll over when he tried to walk, and his front paws doubled up under him, and his eyes were dull and blind. So I went off in a train to find a Trusty Taxidermist (this means a man who knows about animals' insides) and I found him in a museum (curiously enough he was stuffing a lion that very day), and I said: "We have a baby lion who weighs five pounds seven ounces, but he doesn't thrive. His hind legs are weak, and he rolls over when he tries to walk. What shall we do?"

"You must give him broth," said the Trusty Taxidermist. "Milk isn't enough for him. Give him mutton broth at eight in the morning and four in the afternoon; you must also buy a dandy brush—same as they brush horses with—and brush him every day to make up for his own Mummy not being able to lick him with her tongue."

So we bought a dandy brush (a good hard one) and mutton for broth, and we gave him the broth from the bottle, and in two days he was a different lion. His hind legs grew stronger, and his eyes grew lighter, and his furry, wooly skin grew cleaner, and we all said: "Now we must give him a real name of his own." We inquired into his family history and found that his parents were both Matabele lions from the far north, and that the Matabele word for lion was 'umslibaan, but we called him Sullivan for short; and that very day he knocked a bit of skin off his nose trying to climb the wire fence of the den. Then he began to play with Daniel and Una—specially Una, who walked all round the garden hugging him till he squeaked, and Daniel used to brush him with the dandy brush.

One day Una went into the den as usual and put her hand into Sullivan's house to drag him out, just as usual, and Sullivan flattened his little black-tipped ears back to his thick wooly head and opened his mouth and said: "Ough! Ough! Ough!" like a baboon. Una came out very quick and said: "I think Sullivan has teeth. Come and look." We saw that he had six or eight very pretty little teeth about a quarter of an inch long, and we said: "Why should we give up our time to feeding this Monarch of the Jungle (that is a grown-up name for lion) every few hours through a feeding bottle? Let him feed himself." In those days he weighed eight pounds eight ounces, and he could run and jump and growl but he did not like to feed himself.

For two days he wouldn't feed himself at all. He sang for his supper, like little Tommy Tucker, and he sang for his breakfast and his dinner, making noises deep in his chest—high noises and low noises and coughing noises. Una was very distressed. She ran about saying: "Ah, do please let the lion have his bottle! He aren't fit to be weaned."

Daniel, who doesn't speak plain, would go off to the Lion's Den, where poor Sullivan sat looking at a plate of cold broth, and he would say: "Tullibun, Tullibun, eat up all yo' dinner or you'll be hungry."

But at last Sullivan made up his mind that bottles would never come again, and he put down his little nose and ate for dear life. I was told later that Both Babies' Mummy had been out in the early morning and dipped her finger in mutton broth and coaxed Sullivan to lick it off, and she discovered that his tongue was as raspy as a file. Then we were sure he ought to feed himself.

So we weaned Sullivan, and he weighed ten

pounds two ounces, and the truly happy times of his life began. Every morning Una and Daniel would let him out of the den. He was perfectly polite so long as no one put his hand into his house: he would come out at a steady, rocking-horse can-ter that looked slow, but was quicker even than Una's run. Then he would be brushed with the dandy brush, first on his yellow tummy, and then on his yellow back, and then under his yellow chin, and then on his dark yellow mane. The mane hair of a baby lion is a little thicker than the rest of his hair, and Sullivan's was tinged with black. A man who had shot a good many lions told us that Sullivan was a "genuine black Matabele lion," and would grow into a regular beauty.

After his brush he would come out into the garden to watch Daniel and Una swing; or he would hoist himself up on the stoop to watch Both Babies' Mummy sew, or he would go into my room and lie under a couch. If I wished to get rid of him I had to call Una, for at her voice he would solemnly trundle out and help her chase butterflies among the hydrangeas; he never took any notice of me.

One of the many queer things about him was the way he matched his backgrounds— like the leopard on the High Veldt. He would lie down on the bare full glare of the sun, tiled stoop in the and you could step on him before you saw him; he would sit in the shadow of a wall or slide into a garden-border and till he moved you could not tell that he was there.

Sudden noises, like banging doors, always annoyed him. He would go straight backward and almost as fast as he ran forward till he got his back up against a wall or a shrub, and there he would lift one little, broad paw and look wicked till he heard Una or Daniel call him. If he smelt anything on the wind he would stop quite still and lift his head high into the air, very slowly till he had quite made up his mind. Then he would most slowly steal down wind with his tail switching a trifle at the very end. The first time he played with a ball he struck it, just as his grandfather must have struck at the big Matabele oxen in the far north—one paw above and one paw below, with a wrench and a twist—and the ball bounced over his shoulder. He could use his paws as easily as a man can use his arms and much

more quickly. He always turned his back on you when he was examining anything; and that was a signal that you were not to interfere with him.

We used to believe that little lions were only big cats, as the books say; but Sullivan taught us that lions are always lions. He would play in his own way at his own games; but he never chased his tail or patted a cork and string or did any foolish, kitten tricks. He never forgot that he was a lion—not a dog, nor a cat, but a lion, and the son of a lion. When he lay down he would cross his paws and look like the big carved lions in Trafalgar Square; when he rose up and sniffed he looked like the lions that a man called Barye used to make in bronze; and when he lifted one paw and opened his mouth and wrinkled up his nose to be angry (as he did when we washed him all over with carbolic and water, because of fleas) he looked like the lion that the old Assyrians drew on stone.

He never did anything funny; he was never silly or amusing (not even when he had been dipped in carbolic and water), and he never behaved as though he were trying to show off. Kittens do.

He kept himself to himself more and more as he grew older, and one day—I shall never forget it—he began to see out of his eyes. Up till then they had been dull and stupid—just like a young baby's eyes. But that day—I saw them first under my couch— they were grown-up lion's eyes—soft and blazing at the same time, without a wink in them, eyes that seemed to look right through you and out over all Africa. Though he had been born in captivity, like Alice, his mummy, and Induna, his father, and though the only home he had ever known was on the slopes of the big mountain where Africa ended, we never once saw him look up the hill when he lay down to do his solemn, serious thinking. He always faced squarely to the north, to the great open plains and the ragged, jagged mountains beyond them—looking up and into the big, sunny, dry Africa that had once belonged to his people.

That was very curious. He would think and he would sigh—just exactly like a man. He was full of curious, half-human noises—little grunts and groans and mutters and mumbles.

Well, this is really the end of the tale, Best Beloved. He grew to weigh more than fifteen pounds when we had to leave him. We were very proud of this, and triumphed over the Keeper man and the other people who had said that we could never bring him up by hand, and they said: "You've certainly won the game. You can have this lion if you like and take him home and give him to the zoo." But we said: "No. Sullivan is one of the family, and if he were taken to a cold, wet, foggy zoo he'd die. Let him stay here where we can find him when we come back. Let him have the cage near his mummy, where the Australian Dingo-dog lives, and next year we'll see if he remembers Daniel and Una and the feeding bottle."

So they said they would do all those things, and we came away leaving Sullivan close upon sixteen pounds' weight, in perfect health with the beginnings of a beautiful mane.

I like to think of him up the hill in the sunshine, with his paws crossed, looking north—always north, straight up over all Africa.

Oh, Budge, the brindled bull-pup? Before Sullivan was weaned a man took Budge away to make a real bulldog of him. Besides, Sullivan needed all the house to sleep in.

The American-born Mrs. Kipling was very much the capable, determined "Mummy" who could cope with a pet lion.

OLD TIMES WITH THE CIRCUS
by Kin Hubbard

Frank Hyatt joined the circus in 1863 and he continued traveling with tent shows until his retirement in 1920, at which time he was manager of the Barnum & Bailey show. He was 83 in 1923, when this account of his career appeared in the Post. *Author Hubbard is remembered as creator of a humorous backwoods character, Abe Martin.*

This is the story of the wagon circus, which began in America, in an important way for the period, in 1815, and continued until the '70s, at which time associates of the late P. T. Barnum prevailed upon him to permit the use of his name in the exploitation of a show with which he had really no direct connection—barring the 3 percent of the gross receipts which he extracted for the use of the magic trademark, Barnum's Greatest, and so on.

Of those who entertained the masses under white tents before and after the advent of covered wagons, the days of the forty-niners, and other epoch-making periods of American history, few remain to tell the story of the days when circus life was anything but a primrose path of dalliance. It was a time of pioneers and heroes; a time, for instance, when there was no rebellion in camp when it became known to performers that a period of one month would be consumed in making a journey halfway across the country to the place of opening; a time when the cry of "Hey, Rube!" was first heard in the land, during the period immediately preceding and after the war between the states; when there were no Pullmans to transport stars of the big top; when all were content to take pot luck with the hospitality of farmers, as they went their way; and when the routes of the circuses were outlined by advance agents—literally path-finders—who placed fence rails and clumps of bushes along the line, to guide the caravans that followed with the troupes of performers and dens of animals.

It has been many years since the spangled entertainers, along with gaudily attired but less important—from an entertainment viewpoint—members of a touring circus stopped on their way within a few miles of a one-night stand, left their bunks in the passenger wagons and gaily bedecked themselves for the big parade, the glittering Oriental spectacle, which invariably incited interest in the performances to which admission was charged. Yet this sort of thing was very common and is remembered by retired showmen and performers.

"In traveling over an agricultural country we had many pathfinders," says Mr. Hyatt. "One man would go ahead six or eight weeks in advance, to arrange for the feeding of the animals, about 175 head of horses in addition to the wild beasts. Then there was another pathfinder, or advance agent, who would go two weeks ahead of the show, reporting specifically on every turn in the road. Finally followed the twenty-four-hour man, who would leave the circus grounds at ten o'clock at night and go ahead on the route we were to follow. He would either take a rail or pile up grass, to indicate which way we were to go, and would mark the dangerous places with red lanterns, which the driver of the last wagon would gather up. We would have breakfast at one o'clock in the morning, after the tents were prepared for the journey. The baggage wagons always went ahead, and then came the animal wagons. In traveling through the Western country—

Kansas, for instance—we used the compass for laying out our route.

"My first actual circus experience was in taking care of a giraffe in 1863. I had just come out of the Army, having been attached to the Duryea Zouaves. The giraffe was then regarded as an exceedingly rare animal. Indeed, this was the second imported to this country. The animal was taken off a ship and placed in a high cage especially built for it. Six horses were attached to the wagon upon which the cage was placed, and I had a man to drive the wagon. The giraffe was consigned to the Van Amberg show in Cleveland, Ohio. We had as opposition in Cleveland the Sands & Nathan shows, and one of the featured attractions of their outfit was the first hippopotamus ever brought to this country. He wasn't larger than an ordinary hog, but the country was flooded with posters calling attention to the 'animal that sweats blood.'

"I suppose a journey of twenty-nine days over a rugged country, covering mountains and through waters, ought to furnish material for a story within itself; but looking back over that first trip with the giraffe, which I personally conducted from New York to Cleveland, I can't recall anything out of the ordinary. The trip didn't seem to me at all monotonous. It was a bit lonesome, having only the driver of the wagon conveying the giraffe to converse with; but we took turns about driving. I would drive for a few hours and then keep company with the giraffe, or walk along the side of the wagon.

"While with the Van Amberg circus in 1868, starting from Carthage, Illinois, we crossed the river at Keokuk while the Indian massacre was a topic of discussion. Our advertising brigade, on the way to Topeka, Kansas, had been driven back by United States troops, but there were other conditions besides the uprising of the Indians, which were giving cause for grave concern even to the casual traveler. I was manager of the Van Amberg circus at the time and was warned to get across the Pottawatomie River. Foolishly I drove back to Keokuk to get a one-o'clock breakfast before starting. The boss hostler was with me, and the river was so low we didn't think there could be any danger. After we had come back from our early breakfast we could see that the warnings given us had been well advised, for the river was beginning to fill up. I directed that one bareback man who could swim should proceed, with others carrying torches to guide us across the river. The leaders of the caravan led the way for our animals, swimming their way across the Pottawatomie River. With every cage of animals came a rider on horseback to steady and keep them afloat, and we finally got across after several of our men had lost their lives in the struggle against the elements.

"In the days of the wagon circus we slept in the open and under canvas. Nobody went to hotels except featured performers, but we had the best food in the land that money could buy, and all that we could ever eat at that. There was no stinting. We could pass the plate around for the second time. Beef, chickens and vegetables were part of our daily menu. In the Western country, in Kansas and Nebraska, where game was plentiful, we were never at a loss for headliners on the menu so long as we had good sharpshooters with the show. They would supply us with prairie chickens and venison. We didn't travel on Sunday. That was a day of recreation, but fishing and hunting were not considered out of line.

"I remember on one occasion we broke our journey from one town to the other in a hamlet on the side of a stream in Kansas. There was plenty of good water. We stopped at noon, shortly after which time a lot of wagons drove up. We soon found that we were mixed up with a crowd of Baptists who had a ceremony underway which required water and plenty of it. They baptized several candidates, and in the service all of our boys joined. Later a collection was taken up and I rather think more money was gathered than in church.

"In Western Missouri and Kansas, which we covered in those days, the feeling engendered by the war ran high, and there was hardly a day when there weren't fights between the town people and the show people. These fights usually started with fists and wound up with the use of clubs, and sometimes there were shooting affairs.

"One of the earliest of the wagon shows in what was known as the flat-foot party was the June, Titus & De Angeline circus, which wintered at farms in and around Brewster, New York.

"George Bailey, of Danbury, Connecticut, was associated with Lew June and De Angeline in this enterprise. It was a circus and also a menagerie. This is the firm that brought the first elephant

Magic on Main Street. The circus parade brought 19th-century rural America all it knew of glamour and grandeur.

to America from Bombay, India, in a sailing ship and landed him at Fall River in Massachusetts. In lieu of a tent they used to travel with him by night and show him during the day in the tavern barns, out of which grew the famous alibi, 'I have been down to see the elephant.'

"Hannibal and Tippo Sahib were the two biggest elephants to be quartered during winter months at Connersville. Each had tusks eight feet long. We see nothing like them these days. There was another old elephant called Bolivar that George Johnson used to handle in Philadelphia. Bolivar got on a rampage at his winter quarters and had everybody and every animal hunting for cover. Johnson, who hadn't seen the elephant for years, happened along and there was a joyous reunion. Bolivar became as docile as a lamb under the spell of his old master's presence and voice. We carried coach dogs to keep the elephants on their good behavior. The elephants were afraid of these little barking pests and would run from them quicker than they would from anything else.

"Each show was equipped with a saddler's outfit to make repairs, a blacksmith's shop and a harness-repairing department. We made our own harness. It was quite an art to drive horses in squads of six and ten, with the whip as the principal persuader. The experienced driver held the lines with one hand to check the horses, with the other in control of the whip. Whenever a new fellow would come along asking for a job as driver, the boss hostler would ask, 'Where in hell's your whip?'

"Jimmy Robinson was the first bareback rider. He was a half brother to the first Uncle John Robinson, originator of the first John Robinson circus. Jimmy did a straight riding act without any frills or acrobatic capers. Then came Willie O'Dale, who startled the crowds with his thrilling back somersault. Then came Madame Dockrill, a Frenchwoman, who was one of the stars of the London Circus and who drew the fabulous sum—as it was regarded at the time, for the work performed—of 250 dollars a week. Hers, too, was a straight bareback-riding stunt, with an added thrill when she jumped through a hoop of fire.

"Madame Cordelia was the first to jump through a hoop of fire with gleaming daggers protruding from the hoop, to give an added hazard to the act. Robert Stickney, the handsome, graceful, polished Adonis of the arena, was the first pad rider to appear in the circus ring. He was for many years the equestrian star of the John Robinson circus. Stickney maintained his individual supremacy as a rider before and after many other performers of his class had come and gone.

"The highest salary ever paid to a circus performer in my time was paid Dan Rice, of Erie, Pennsylvania, who began his circus career with the Bill Lake show during the period of the war between the states. He drew a thousand dollars a week from the Forepaugh show as the principal clown of that organization. Rice was a Shakespearean clown and his wise cracks were nearly always quotations from Shakespeare. He did one turn during the course of the show and was accorded all the honors and courtesies that would be lavished on a prima donna in a hall show. Another famous Shakespearean clown, who followed Dan Rice, was Pete Conklin, brother of George Conklin, a famous animal trainer.

"In 1870 two of the greatest tented aggregations then traveling, the Adam Forepaugh show and the New York circus, exhibited in my native town, then a village of twenty-five hundred souls, on the same day. The rivalry and boasting were perhaps the greatest in the history of the tented arena. Adam Forepaugh addressed a card to "citizens and strangers," in which he offered to forfeit ten thousand dollars if he did not have the most wonderful herd—three—of trained elephants in existence. He also cut his admission fee in half. The New York circus offered to wager ten thousand dollars that no other circus in the world could produce a wonderful cynocephalus, an equestrian ape. For weeks the town was almost shut off from the world by circus billboards. Even the courthouse was left with only one small entrance, and the courtroom had to use lamps for three weeks while posters covered all the windows.

"The Barnum circus opened on April 10, 1871, in Brooklyn, New York, with more men, animals and horses, it was claimed, than any previous tent show. Admiral Dot the Eldorado Elf, the Palestine Giant, Esau the Bearded Boy, Anna Lenke the

Armless Wonder, the Fiji cannibals and a giraffe were widely advertised features. In transporting the show in the old-fashioned way, in wagons drawn by horses, it was often necessary to play small towns, to make jumps overnight. Mr. Coup reasoned that with the receipts ranging from five to seven thousand dollars in the larger cities visited, and falling to two thousand dollars in the smaller cities, it would pay in the long run to transport the show by rail, and arrangements were made with the railroad people to that effect.

"Thus the Barnum show became a railroad circus, over, however, the protest of the great showmen."

At night, flares lent sparkle to smiles, spangles, hid all evidence of mud, dust, wear and tear.

JOSEPHINE, THE TAME WILD BOAR

by Albert Schweitzer

In some ways he was St. Francis come again to preach by example to a materialistic 20th-century world his doctrine of humility, altruism, and reverence for life. It is said that he regretted having to kill flies and mosquitoes at his jungle hospital, and that he regarded even microorganisms—germs—as fellow creatures with a right to life in God's world. That was one Albert Schweitzer—the idealist, the theologian and philosopher. In this selection we meet another Dr. Schweitzer—the pragmatist. Which is the better portrait of a remarkable man who turned his back on a distinguised career as musician and author to serve humanity?

One day a Negro woman brought me a tame wild boar about two months old.

"It is called Josephine, and it will follow you around like a dog," she said.

We agreed upon five francs as the price. My wife was just then away for a few days. With the help of Joseph and N'Kendju, my hospital assistant, I immediately drove some stakes into the ground and made a pen, with the wire netting rather deep in the earth. Both of my black helpers smiled.

"A wild boar will not remain in a pen; it digs his way out from under it," said Joseph.

"Well, I should like to see this little wild boar get under this wire netting sunk deep in the earth," I answered.

"You will see," said Joseph.

The next morning the animal had already gotten out. I felt almost relieved about it, for I had promised my wife that I would make no new acquisition to our zoo without her consent, and I had a foreboding that a boar would not be to her liking.

When I came up from the hospital for the midday meal, however, there was Josephine waiting for me in front of the house, and looking at me as if she wanted to say: "I will remain ever so faithful to you, but you must not repeat the trick with the pen." And so it was.

When my wife arrived she shrugged her shoulders. She never enjoyed Josephine's confidence and never sought it. Josephine had a very delicate sensibility about such things. In time, when she had come to understand that she was not permitted to go up on the veranda, things became bearable. On a Saturday some weeks later, however, Josephine disappeared. In the evening the missionary met me in front of my house and shared my sorrow, since Josephine had also shown some attachment to him.

"I feel sure she has met her end in some cooking pot," he said. "It was inevitable."

With the blacks a wild boar, even when tamed, does not fall within the category of a domestic animal but remains a wild animal that belongs to him who kills it. While he was still speaking Josephine appeared, behind her a Negro with a gun.

"I was standing," he said, "in the clearing, where the ruins of the former American missionary's house are still to be seen, when I saw this wild boar. I was just taking aim, but it came running up to me and rubbed against my legs. An extraordinary wild boar! But imagine what it then did. It trotted away with me after it, and now here we are. So it's your wild boar? How fortunate that this did not happen to a hunter who is not so quick-witted as I." I understood this hint, complimented him generously and gave him a nice present.

But the thought that my wild boar was in constant danger, as the missionary had told me, troubled me, while the two of us were rubbing the back of the newly recovered animal with our feet, something which Josephine greatly loved.

"Listen, doctor," the missionary began suddenly, "tomorrow I have to preach, and as it will soon be necessary to touch upon the sin of theft in every service for our Negroes, I will bring in Josephine right off tomorrow morning as an illustration of the fact that an animal once wild and anybody's property nonetheless may afterwards become private property and inviolable, when it is cherished by someone."

The next morning, in the second half of the sermon, Josephine was introduced. With rapt attention the Negroes listened as the missionary explained the complicated case and broadened the horizon of their notion of property. At that very moment—it made me almost ill—Josephine took her place beside the preacher! In Lambaréné, you know, we have no chancel. The service of worship takes place in the corrugated-iron barrack in which the school is also held. The preacher stands on the ground. The doors are always left open, so that some air can come in. People are quite accustomed to have hens and sheep come and go during the service. The missionary's dogs regularly take part in it.

But that Josephine should also have become religious seemed horrible to me. Moreover, I was soon made forcibly aware that she did not know how to behave. She had come fresh from the marsh, covered with black mire. And now she walked among the benches, where the children sat, while they drew their knees up under their chins! Then she came to the women! Then to the other missionary! Then to the ladies of the mission with their white skirts, trying to rub herself against them! Then to the lady doctor! Then to me! At that moment she received a kick, the first she ever had from me. It was, however, justified.

I was never able to discourage Josephine's delight in the church service. She could not be shut up; neither could she be tied up, for she worked her way out of every harness that I contrived for her. The moment the bell sounded she ran to church. I do not think she missed any of the morning or evening prayers for the children. I proposed to the missionary who was in charge of the station that because of all this I should kill her. But he forbade me to do so; the animal should not lose her life because of such an instinct. In time Josephine began to behave more properly in church.

How shall I sufficiently praise your wisdom, Josephine! To avoid being bothered by gnats at night, you adopted the custom of wandering into the boys' dormitory, and of lying down there under the first good mosquito net. How many times because of this have I had to compensate, with tobacco leaves, those upon whom you forced yourself as a sleeping companion. And when the sand fleas had so grown in your feet that you could no longer walk, you hobbled down to the hospital, let yourself be turned over on your back, endured the knife that the tormentors stuck into your feet, put up with the burning of the tincture of iodine, with which the wounds were daubed, and grunted your sincere thanks when the matter was done with!

"When a wild boar is more than six months old,

it begins to eat hens," N'Kendju stated solemnly.

"Josephine will not go so far as to eat hens," I replied with an unsteady voice.

"She will eat hens, for she is a wild boar," came the response with its inexorable logic. Nonetheless, I ventured to hope.

A Negro came and told me one of his hens was missing. I knew what he meant by this, gave him a gift and told him to be silent.

The lady missionary told me that one of her hens was missing. I knew what she meant by it. But I betrayed nothing, and simply said: "Yes, it is a bad business with the snakes around here." So I forced myself to believe in the innocence of Josephine.

Early one day, however, as I was examining the blood of some patients under the microscope in the hospital, I heard the cackling of hens and through it all the voices of men calling. Shortly thereafter the boy Akaja appeared with a note from the lady doctor. The writing said: "Josephine has gotten in among the chickens, has eaten three of them, and has torn off the tail of the clucking hen. I saw it. You know what you have to do."

I knew it and did it. Josephine was enticed into the hospital, tied up, and expeditiously and artistically slaughtered. Before noon sounded her life came to an end. I estimate that she was about eight months old.

The bacon was cut into strips and stuck on little sticks which I carefully smoked and dried and put away hermetically sealed in a tin.

Not long after, an official came to consult me and I entertained him at lunch. He got some of the bacon.

"What? Smoked bacon? A rarity in this land."

"Sir, it comes from a tame wild boar. I had to kill it because it was eating hens."

"You had a tame wild boar? I had one also which I brought up with a nursing bottle. It cost me many a tin of Swiss milk. But it ran after me like a dog. Unfortunately it was stolen from me. I had given it the name of Josephine."

"In that case, my dear sir, you are now eating the bacon of the tame wild boar that you brought up on the nursing bottle. The woman who sold it to me had stolen it from you."

RASCAL MAKES TROUBLE

by Sterling North

This selection is from the book Rascal: A Memoir of a Better Era. *The era referred to is the time of World War I; the locale is a small town in Wisconsin where North lived alone with his father after his mother's death. Under what other circumstances would a 12-year-old be allowed to sleep with a raccoon and build a canoe in the living room?*

All raccoons are attracted by shining objects, and Rascal was no exception. He was fascinated by brass doorknobs, glass marbles, my broken Ingersoll watch, and small coins. I gave him three bright new pennies which he hoarded with the happiness of a little miser. He felt them carefully, smelled them, tasted them, and then hid them in a dark corner with some of his other treasures. One day he decided to carry one of his pennies to the back porch. Poe-the-Crow was perched on the porch rail teasing the cats, but keeping just beyond their reach. This raucous old bird, who cawed and cussed in crow language, was arching his wings and strutting like a poolroom bully as Rascal pushed open the screen and trundled into the sunlight, his penny shining like gold.

Poe and Rascal had taken an instant dislike to each other when first they met. Crows, like most other birds, know that raccoons steal birds' eggs and sometimes eat fledglings. In addition Poe was jealous. He had seen me petting and pampering my small raccoon. But Rascal was large enough now to pull a few tail feathers from the big black bird during their noisy squabbles. And Poe, who was no fool, was taking few chances.

The penny, however, was so tempting that the crow threw caution to the winds and made a dive for the bright object (for crows are as insatiably attracted by glittering trinkets as are raccoons, and in addition are inveterate thieves).

Rascal was carrying the penny in his mouth, and when Poe swooped to conquer, his beak closed not only on the penny but upon half a dozen of Rascal's coarse, strong whiskers. When the black thief

tried to make his fast getaway he found himself attached to the raccoon, who with a high scream of fury began fighting for his property and his life. Such a tangle of shining black feathers and furious fur you have seldom seen as Rascal and Poe wrestled and struggled. I arrived to untangle them, and both were angry with me. Rascal nipped me slightly for the first time, and Poe made several ungracious comments.

The penny, meanwhile, had rolled from the porch into the grass below, where the crow promptly spotted it, seized it once again, and took wing. "Straight as a crow flies" seldom applied to my wily pet. After any thievery he would travel by devious routes before slipping between the wide slats of the Methodist belfry where he presumably stored his loot.

I gave the incident no more thought, pacified Rascal with another penny, and resumed work on my canoe in the living room.

The blueprint I had made in the manual training shop at school called for a trim and streamlined craft, eighteen feet long and twenty-eight inches wide. The slender longitudinal ribs were fastened at prow and stern and curved around cross-sectional forms between. These and the inner keel were now in place. But the ribs to encircle the craft from gunwale to gunwale presented a problem. I had tried steaming hickory for this purpose, and curving the wood under pressure, but had given it up as an impossible job with my limited equipment.

Then a happy thought struck me. Nothing is tougher than the water elm used in making cheese boxes. An additional convenience is the fact that these cylinders of thin wood are already curved into a complete circle. Most of the tradesmen were friends of mine. They bought the neatly tied bunches of white-tipped, crimson radishes which I raised, and gave me meat scraps and stale loaves of bread for Wowser. I was sure they would give me empty cheese boxes if I asked politely.

At Pringle's they had one good cheese box and at Wilson's grocery another. Before I had visited half the food stores in town I had all I needed. At home in the living room I marked two-inch strips on each of these cylinders, and with my father's best ripsaw began the exacting and exasperating job of cutting the featherweight canoe ribs. Some of the boxes split and were ruined. But with patience I finally sawed the forty-two circles that were required. I found to my great joy that these strips of wood had no tendency to spread, but on the contrary held their circular shape to perfection.

All of this work in the living room created some disorder, particularly when I began sandpapering the ribs, starting with number-two sandpaper and finishing with double 0, which is very fine. The wood smoothed to a satin surface, creamy yellow and pleasant to the touch.

I was still sanding the ribs, with Rascal clambering over the unfinish-

ed canoe, when a Stutz Bearcat curved up the gravel drive. Out stepped my beautiful sister Theodora Maud (the Maud from Tennyson of course). With her was one of her maids, and Theo had a determined look on her patrician face and a light in her eyes that went well with her auburn hair.

"Theo, Theo!" I shouted happily, running out to embrace her.

"Hello, sonny boy—my, you're all covered with sawdust."

"Well, you see, Theo, I'm building a canoe."

"That's nice, but where?"

"In the living room," I said, dropping my eyes.

"Merciful heavens!" Theo said. "Now help Jennie with the luggage, and put it in the downstairs bedroom."

I didn't dare tell Theo that I was sleeping in that room and that Rascal slept there too. I loved this sister but I was slightly in awe of her. She had been kind to me after Mother died, and she would be kind to me again some years later when I was stricken by infantile paralysis. But she was a martinet concerning deportment, dress, housekeeping, and much besides. It was her training that made me jump up like a jack-in-the-box whenever an older person, particularly a lady, entered the room. She dressed me on occasion in such fashionable Norfolk

Hand-raising a baby raccoon is not difficult and the animal makes an affectionate and interesting pet.

suits and jackets that it took several fist fights to prove I was still one of the gang.

Theo gave the living room one sweeping glance and raised her hands in horror.

"I've never seen such a mess in my life," she said.

"I sweep up the sawdust and shavings every evening."

"Yes, I see them, right there in the fireplace."

"Daddy and I do a good job of batching it," I said defensively.

"Batching it! That's just the trouble," Theo said severely. "Now you get that canoe out of the living room this minute, Sterling."

I had a little of the family's fire, so I replied with a firm and angry refusal. I told Theo we were living exactly the way we wanted to live, and that I would never wear a Norfolk suit or a necktie again except on Sundays.

"You're not too big to spank," Theo said, her lovely eyes flashing.

"You just try."

"Now, Sterling, I've brought Jennie to clean this house from top to bottom. I'll cook some decent food. We'll hire a full-time housekeeper, and we'll get this canoe out of the living room."

"Can't you just leave us alone?" I said mournfully. "Anyhow, Theo, you're not my mother."

"Oh, sonny

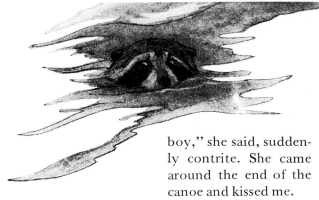

boy," she said, suddenly contrite. She came around the end of the canoe and kissed me.

Giving Theo the downstairs bedroom didn't worry *me*. She always took this big room with its adjoining bath. She said none of the other beds was fit to sleep in.

My difficulty would come in trying to explain all this to Rascal. Raccoons have definite patterns in their minds, and Rascal had decisively chosen the same bed that Theo wanted. He also preferred a room with a bath. Each evening I closed the drain of the big lavatory and left a few inches of water in the basin so that Rascal could get a drink at any time during the night, or perhaps wash a cricket before he ate it. How was I to reveal to this small creature of habit that he was being evicted?

Theo had not seen Rascal until this moment. He had been lying low, watching and listening shrewdly. He may not have been a perfect judge of character, but he reacted with surprising sensitivity to various modulations of voice. He knew when he was being praised or scolded and when people were feeling affectionate or angry. He didn't altogether

The adult raccoon is not *a good pet. Sterling North eventually took Rascal deep into a wilderness area and set him free.*

trust this auburn-haired stranger, although his eyes strayed often to her shining hair.

His virtual invisibility was due to the fact that he was lying on a large jaguar-skin rug which Uncle Justus had sent us from Pará, Brazil. The mounted head had realistic glass eyes which Rascal often fondled and sometimes tried to dislodge. The little raccoon blended perfectly into the handsomely marked pelt of the once ferocious jungle cat.

When Rascal began to rise from that skin, like the disembodied spirit of the Amazonian jaguar, it startled Theo nearly out of her wits.

"What in the world is *that*?"

"That's Rascal, my good little raccoon."

"You mean it lives in the house?"

"Only part of the time."

"Does it bite?"

"Not unless you slap him or scold him."

"Now get that thing right out of here, Sterling."

"Well, all right," I agreed reluctantly, knowing that Rascal could let himself back in any time he pleased.

Rascal spent the rest of the day sleeping in the oak tree, but that night when the moon arose, he backed down his tree, padded to the screen door, opened it with ease, and went confidently to our bedroom and crawled in with Theo. My father and I, who were sleeping upstairs, were awakened by a bloodcurdling yell. We rushed downstairs in our pajamas to find Theo standing on a chair, treed by a complacent little raccoon who sat on the floor below blinking up at this crazy human being who was screeching like a fire siren.

"He always sleeps in this bed," I explained. "He's harmless and perfectly clean."

"You take that horrid little animal out of the house this minute," Theo ordered, "and hook the screen door so it can't possibly get back in."

"Well, OK," I said, "but you're sleeping in Rascal's bed. And he has just as many rights around here as you have."

"Don't be impertinent," Theo said.

A later episode of this visit is worth recalling. Recently married, Theo treasured her engagement ring, a square-cut diamond of perhaps one carat, mounted in white gold. She had misplaced this ring on several occasions. Once we dug up eighty-five feet of sewer, only to find that she had transferred the ring to another purse.

True to form, she again lost her ring. She thought she had left it on the wide rim of the lavatory when she went to bed, and that either it had fallen into the drain or had been stolen. No one in Brailsford Junction ever locked his door. Not within memory had there been a robbery.

We ransacked the house, hunted through the grass and the flower beds, and then made plans for again digging up the sewer. Then a farfetched possibility struck me like a bolt from the blue. Just before dawn on that fateful morning I had heard Rascal and Poe having a terrible fight on the back porch. Before I could shake the sleep from my eyes, the cawing and screaming subsided and I had drowsed off again.

Feeling as keen as a Scotland Yard detective, I began to weave a theory. On this fourth night of Theo's visit I had not hooked the screen door. Rascal apparently had slipped into the house, reached the downstairs bedroom, and wisely chosen not to create another scene. He had decided, however, to have a drink of fresh water from the lavatory, had climbed to the windowsill and then to the basin, and found it empty. But joy of joys, there on the lavatory was the prettiest object he had ever seen in his life, a big diamond ring gleaming with blue-white radiance in the pre-dawn light.

If my theory were sound, Rascal had picked up the ring and taken it to the back porch where Poe-the-Crow had spotted the treasure. This would explain the crow-raccoon fight.

Quite probably the black thief had won again—at least in the matter of flying away with the loot.

I had to ask permission of the kindly Reverend Hooton before starting my dusty climb to the seventy-five-foot belfry. The shaft was dark and filled with cobwebs and some of the cleats were loose, making me fear I might fall. But having enlisted in this venture, I could not turn back. At long last I reached the airy little room at the top, with its widely spaced shutters, furnishing a view of the town and the creek winding toward the river. I stood for a few moments viewing the world below me. Then I touched the big deep-toned bell which had tolled forty-seven times for my mother and would one day toll ninety-nine times for my father.

Remembering my mission, I began to search the dusty belfry. Behind a pile of discarded hymnals which some dedicated idiot had lugged to this unlikely storage place I found the ragged circle of twigs and leaves and black feathers which Poe-the-Crow called home. As some people keep their money in their mattress, Poe had made his bed even more uncomfortable with a pile of shining junk which overran the nest and spilled across the floor. Here were glassies and steelies and one real agate marble, all of which he had stolen during our marble games. Here was my football whistle, snatched while he hovered just over the line of scrimmage shouting, "What fun! What fun!" Here were scraps of sheet copper, a second key to our Oldsmobile, and, wonder of wonders, Theo's diamond ring.

Poe dropped in at about this time, and he didn't say, "What fun!" He wouldn't let me pet him, and he cawed and swore at me as though *I* were the thief and *he* the honest householder.

I put several of these stolen articles into my pocket, my best marbles, the second key to our car, my football whistle, and Theo's ring, of course. But I left many of the shining trinkets, knowing that Poe couldn't tell sheet copper from a diamond ring. The crow's raucous criticism followed me all the way down that shaft and out into the sunlight.

Theo was so pleased at my recovery of her ring that she did not insist on the removal of my canoe from the living room. And she postponed the decision concerning a full-time housekeeper. She merely fed us delightful meals, and, with Jennie's help, left the house shining clean, with fresh curtains at the windows. Then with a good-bye kiss and a wave of her hand she was off again.

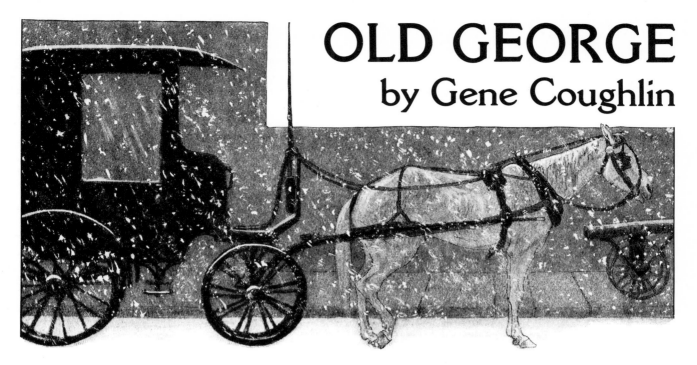

OLD GEORGE
by Gene Coughlin

Newspaperman Coughlin grew up in Illinois and Indiana, worked on papers in Joliet, Chicago, Los Angeles and New York, and as a Hollywood press agent. He wrote this memoir for the Post *in 1961.*

This was the third time in an hour that Old George, his ears back and his nostrils flaring, had chased me across the Lake Erie & Western right-of-way and, in many respects, it was the worst rout of the day. I stubbed the big toe of my right foot on a railroad tie and cut the other bare foot on a cinder. Those pains and a shortness of breath made up the physical casualties.

Mentally and spiritually I was as deep in despair as a twelve-year-old could be. A couple of times as I limped along Mill Street, skirting the lush lot where Old George was nonchalantly gobbling up the grass and the weeds, I was tempted to give up the fight and go back home—two blocks away—confess my failure, and let my father or my two older brothers capture the big bay Percheron and take him to the barn. Each time I rejected the idea, because (a) I had volunteered for the assignment of leading him to and from pasture every summer evening and (b) I was really fond of Old George, and I wanted the association to continue. I liked to stroke the fine sheen of his neck and the tremendous muscles of his shoulders and thighs. Especially I liked the feel of the velvety muzzle when he swooshed up an apple or a chunk of brown sugar from my hand and thanked me with a nudge that usually knocked off my cap and left me damp around the head and shoulders, but warm and happy inside.

I knew that, at heart, George was gentle and good-natured; that he liked humans, particularly children. Every evening when Delt McGill drove him home from the coalyard, George would halt in front of our house without being told and wait while a half-dozen small boys and girls got hoisted onto his back.

Then, and only then, would he break into a trot, the empty wagon clattering behind him as he took the yelling passengers around the block. Back at the starting point he would stand motionless while they were unloaded, turning his huge head as though counting them, and resume his normal plodding pace as he headed for the barn.

Old George had the barn to himself at this time, 1914, and I think that, instead of being lonesome, he was relieved. Dolly wasn't there to nag him. Some nine years earlier when my father turned his back on a successful railroading career in Joliet, Illinois, and started the Coughlin Coal & Ice Company in Tipton, Indiana—a town of 4,000 forty miles north of Indianapolis—my uncle, Mike Hoffman, had obtained George and Dolly to do the hauling.

Dolly was a beautiful white mare with delusions of grandeur picked up on the farm where she had been foaled. Delt McGill, who did the loading and delivering of the coal and—very rarely of late—the ice, swore that Dolly acted as if she were too good for the coalyard and for us; her ambition was to be a circus performer, Delt said, or at least to pull a gaudy brewery wagon with other prancing horses.

When they were first hitched as a team, she made life miserable for Old George, snorting and snapping at him and, when she discovered his neuter gender, ridiculing him. Two things combined to bring about the sale of Dolly to a farmer near Hobbs: the falling off of business to the extent that a single horse could do the work and, secondly, Dolly's ingratitude when my father made her a canvas raincoat and hood. She didn't want any part of it and, when he tried to pull the hood down over her ears, Dolly stepped on his foot.

Dolly left the next day, and everyone felt better, George especially.

For seven months of the year George was meek and mild, as a gelding should be; but with the coming of spring and the green vegetation he underwent a change. He became, he thought, a complete horse, a transformation I did not understand at the time. From April to September he had very little coal to haul, and he had to have an outlet for his pent-up vitality; he found it in eating. Old George was a glutton, frustrated during the cold months when hay and oats were rationed, for economic reasons, but indulging in one long orgy from late spring to late summer, when free grass flourished on the vacant lots near our house and barn.

After the day's work and the ride for the small fry, Delt unhitched him at the barn behind our house, and John and Joe, my older brothers, took turns leading him to the lot he currently favored. The summer I was twelve, both brothers had jobs, and I asked for the privilege of escorting Old George. My father, Owen, was dubious at first; largely, I suppose, because of the disparity in size and weight. I weighed something under 100 pounds; George a very little something under 2,000 pounds.

"Please, pop!" I pleaded as my father rubbed his mustache. "I can handle him. We understand each other!"

"Wel-l-l, you do seem to get along together. You'll have to watch him, or he'll make a pig of himself. If he eats too much grass, he'll get the colic. Give him an hour, maybe a little longer." He put a loose halter on George and handed me the coil of rope attached to the nose strap.

"I bet I won't even need the rope," I bragged. "Hey, George?"

George whinnied softly and nudged me. We were pals, and we remained pals for the first fifty minutes or so. When I learned from a passerby on Mill Street that the hour was almost up, I clucked and walked confidently toward him. He kept on cropping noisily, until I was some forty feet from him. Then he snorted, reared up on his hind feet, trumpeted like a wild stallion and came charging at me! This was not the Old George that delighted in treating children to a ride, not the gentle George that rubbed his soft nose against my coat pockets in search of apples and sugar. This was a total stranger, a fire-breathing beast with flaming eyes. I turned tail and fled in panic.

I do not know how far he pursued me but, when I looked back from the other side of the Lake Erie & Western tracks, he was grazing placidly again. I told myself I must have frightened him by my approach; I should have used the rope and worked my way toward him slowly. When my breath came back, I tried that method, making sweet talk as I advanced, but the reaction was the same. Again he reared and charged, and again I ran. After five such performances—his belly distended and his legs tired—he permitted me to pick up the rope and coil it as I advanced, until I had a grip a couple of feet from the halter. Then he lowered his head, nuzzled my ear moistly and let me lead him to the barn. My father pointed out that we had been out more than an hour and a half.

"Was he eating grass all that time?" he inquired.

"No," I said truthfully, "he was exercising."

Next day I felt no qualms about taking him, George, to the lot. The harrowing escapes of the previous evening were pretty well forgotten, or relegated to the department of bad dreams. I turned him loose, read for about an hour and strode out to get him. And it happened again. He reared and charged and even worked up some foam that flew from his lips as I headed for the tracks once more.

He let me take him into custody on the fourth try. The routine was repeated daily for more than a week, up until this fateful day of the stubbed toe and the cut foot—the day of decision.

I turned off Mill Street into the alley bordering the grazing lot on the south and glared at Old George through tear-smarting eyes. Then, to complete my humiliation, I heard a familiar voice: "Made you skedaddle again, didn't he, boy?"

I didn't have to turn around to know it was grandpa Emeheiser, our best-known Civil War hero and storyteller. He was sitting on the back porch of his cottage, his cane between his knees, his blue Union field hat on his white-topped head, and wearing a smile that turned up the corners of his silvery mustache.

Horse power. With it, horse personality and horse intelligence. Some delivery horses learned routes, hardly needed drivers.

Before I could answer he went on, "Been watchin' for three, four days, now. Time to stop this business. That big fellow out there eatin' himself sick is nothing but a bully, a big bluff. No more runnin' for you, boy. Walk right up to him and call his bluff. Stand yore ground, boy! You hear?"

I heard, and I started down the narrow path that led to the grass. The path went through brier and bramble patches, plus some prickly berry bushes— painful reminders to stay in the lane if you were barefooted. Old George didn't wait for me to come onto the arena, the green grass. While I was still on the path—a good fifty feet from him—he went into his familiar act and came at me like an avenging

freight train. Instinctively, I turned—and bumped into grandpa Emeheiser, who spun me around to face the foe.

"Stand yore ground!" he roared, brandishing his cane. "I'm right here with you, boy!"

I had no choice but to watch the oncoming George, in fear and fascination. And this time it was his turn to panic. Midway in his charge the enormity of what he was about to do, or might have done earlier in the week, seemed to strike him.

It could have been the waving of grandpa's cane; it could have been the realization that he was picking on a small boy and an old man. Whatever the motivation, he tried to stop—I doubt that he

143

could have swerved and missed us—but his ton of flesh had considerable momentum, even in that short distance, and he couldn't apply the brakes standing up.

He sat down suddenly and gave a little squeal as the burs and brambles and cinders met his haunches. He slid to a stop, his forefeet coming to rest a yard from my bare toes and his muzzle on a level with my face.

"Grab his nostrils, boy!" grandpa ordered. "Now! Put your thumb in one and the middle finger in the other and squeeze!"

I extended a trembling hand to George's nose, also trembling, and squeezed.

"Tell him to get up!" grandpa Emeheiser commanded, and I relayed the order. George obeyed, keeping his nostrils down so I could maintain my hold. Grandpa moved around me, took off the halter, coiled the rope and slung it around my neck. During the process George had to sneeze, lifting his head to do so and promptly lowering it again.

"You won't need a rope or halter anymore, boy," grandpa said and slapped George on the shoulder. "He's yore's for keeps now. He'll

Like Pavlov's dogs, firehorses learned to respond to bells. This caused problems for the owners of retired firehorses.

follow you around jus' like a good dog. G'night."

He clumped back to the porch, and I led George home. A couple of times I had to release my grip on his nostrils to flex my thumb and finger, but he kept them handy, just above my right shoulder, so I wouldn't have to reach too far.

My mother and father were out in the backyard, inspecting the tomatoes, when we walked by, headed for the barn. This happened to be one of the times I had let go of George's nose; he was with me on his own.

"What happened?" my father asked. "The rope and halter break?"

"No, sir," I said. "They're all right. I just don't need them anymore. He follows me around like a—like a dog."

I could feel their eyes on me as we went into the barn, George's nose next to my ear. I gave him a salt brick, to ward off colic, and a bucket of water. He stood very still while I put a mixture of Vaseline and axle grease on the scratches where he had sat down so suddenly to avert disaster. I patted his neck, and he gave me a good-night slobber that covered half my shirt.

While my brothers and I were doing the supper dishes that evening, I asked a question that had been bothering me. "Did Old George ever chase you fellows?"

John chuckled. "I never mentioned it," he said, "but I must have run ten miles the first few days I had him out. Then I quit running, and so did he."

Joe smiled slowly. "I learned how to broad-jump the first week," he said. "I got so I could clear the Lake Erie tracks easy. Then I got a stone bruise, and I couldn't run——"

"And you stood your ground?"

They both nodded, and John asked, "Is that what happened to you? You stood your ground today?"

I said, "Yes," put away the last plate and hung up my dish towel.

"Think I'll go swimming," I announced, and they exchanged looks. It was the law in our house that I was not to go near Robinson's gravel pit or Cicero Creek—even in daylight—without one or both of my brothers along.

"I can't go. I've got a date," John said.

"I don't feel like it," Joe put in. "Too tired."

"You don't have to go," I assured them. "I'll go with Tommy and Jody and the rest of my gang."

John sized me up for a few seconds, smiled and said, "I don't see why you shouldn't."

At sixteen he was as tall as my father and muscular, and he nearly filled the doorway leading to the sitting room as he addressed my parents, "Eugene wants to go swimming with Tommy and Jody and the rest of his gang, and I think it's all right. He's a good swimmer, and he's big enough to take care of himself—now."

I could sense my father's objection forming, but he caught the quick glance from my mother and settled back in his chair.

"Well," he said with something like a sigh, "all right. But see that you're home by nine. You hear, Eugene?"

I said I heard and got my cap. Then I remembered something else, and I stopped in the kitchen to borrow a big lump of brown sugar for Old George, my pal.

The horse could be a man's servant—or a boy's friend.

145

MOTHER OF DUCKLINGS
by Konrad Lorenz

Dr. Lorenz was only five when he first played foster mother to a duckling. His lifelong love affair with wild creatures led to the recognition of his field of study as a new branch of science—ethology—defined as the study of comparative behavior of animals.

I was experimenting at one time with young mallards to find out why artificially incubated and freshly hatched ducklings of this species, in contrast to similarly treated greylag goslings, are unapproachable and shy. Greylag goslings unquestioning accept the first living being whom they meet as their mother, and run confidently after him. Mallards, on the contrary, always refused to do this. If I took from the incubator freshly hatched mallards, they invariably ran away from me and pressed themselves in the nearest dark corner. Why? I remembered that I had once let a muscovy duck hatch a clutch of mallard eggs and that the tiny mallards had also failed to accept this foster mother. As soon as they were dry, they had simply run away from her and I had trouble enough to catch these crying, erring children. On the other hand, I once let a fat white farmyard duck hatch out mallards and the little wild things ran just as happily after her as if she had been their real mother. The secret must have lain in her call note, for, in external appearance, the domestic duck was quite as different from a mallard as was the muscovy; but what she had in common with the mallard (which, of course, is the wild progenitor of our farmyard duck) were her vocal expressions. Though, in the process of domestication, the duck has altered considerably in color pattern and body form, its voice has remained practically the same. The inference was clear: I must quack like a mother mallard in order to make the little ducks run after me. No sooner said than done. When, one Whit-Saturday, a brood of pure-bred young mallards was due to hatch, I put the eggs in the incubator, took the babies, as soon as they were dry, under my personal care, and quacked for them the mother's call-note in my best Mallardese. For hours on end I

kept it up, for half the day. The quacking was successful. The little ducks lifted their gaze confidently toward me, obviously had no fear of me this time, and as, still quacking, I drew slowly away from them, they also set themselves obediently in motion and scuttled after me in a tightly huddled group, just as ducklings follow their mother. My theory was indisputably proved. The freshly hatched ducklings have an inborn reaction to the call-note, but not to the optical picture of the mother. Anything that emits the right quack note will be considered as mother, whether it is a fat white Pekin duck or a still fatter man. However, the substituted object must not exceed a certain height. At the beginning of these experiments, I had sat myself down in the grass among the ducklings and, in order to make them follow me, had dragged myself, sitting, away from them. As soon, however, as I stood up and tried, in a standing posture, to lead them on, they gave up, peered searchingly on all sides, but not upward toward me, and it was not long before they began that penetrating piping of abandoned ducklings that we are accustomed simply to call "crying." They were unable to adapt themselves to the fact that their foster mother had become so tall. So I was forced to move along, squatting low, if I wished them to follow me. This was not very comfortable; still less comfortable was the fact that the mallard mother quacks unintermittently. If I ceased for even the space of half a minute from my melodious "Quahg, gegegegeg, Quahg, gegegegeg," the necks of the ducklings became longer and longer, corresponding exactly to "long faces" in human children—and did I then not immediately recommence quacking, the shrill weeping began anew. As soon as I was silent, they seemed to think that I had died, or perhaps

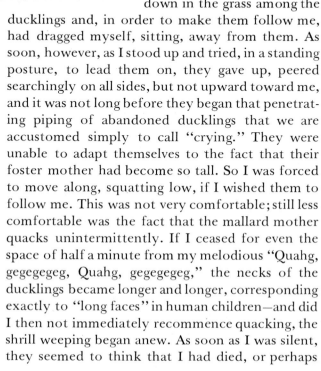

If it is lucky, a newly hatched duckling or chick sees and follows a large moving object that turns out to be its own mother.

that I loved them no more: cause enough for crying! The ducklings, in contrast to the greylag goslings, were most demanding and tiring charges, for, imagine a two-hour walk with such children, all the time squatting low and quacking without interruption! In the interest of science I submitted myself literally for hours on end to this ordeal. So it came about on a certain Whit-Sunday, that, in company with my ducklings, I was wandering about, squatting and quacking, in a May-green meadow at the upper part of our garden. I was congratulating myself on the obedience and exactitude with which

my ducklings came waddling after me, when I suddenly looked up and saw the garden fence framed by a row of dead-white faces; a group of tourists was standing at the fence and staring horrified in my direction.

Forgivable! For all they could see was a big man with a beard dragging himself, crouching, round the meadow, in figures of eight, glancing constantly over his shoulder and quacking—but the ducklings, the all-revealing and all explaining ducklings were hidden in the tall spring grass from the view of the astonished crowd.

147

MY LAST SAFARI
by Robert Ruark

Novelist/journalist/sportsman Ruark knew that the 1962 trip he made into northwestern Kenya would be his last hunt in Africa—his lack of sympathy with emerging African nationalism was well known, and in the future he would no longer be welcome in a part of the world that had become his second and much-loved home. This selection is part of an article that appeared in the Post *in 1963.*

There *was* an elephant in the area of Illaut—not two, not 90, but one. He was a bull, and he was old, very old. His big fresh tracks were corrugated by age, and you could tell by the concentration of his waste that he foraged close by the scanty water in the blinding white sands of the *luga*.

So there was this elephant at Illaut, and Selby and I were drinking coffee in our tentless camp in the middle of the *luga* when Areng, the plum-black Turkana horse wrangler, marched up to the table pushing a scared 10-year-old Samburu-Rendille girl ahead of him.

"This *ndito*, this maiden, says she was off looking for strayed goats this morning, and she was charged by a very big elephant with very big teeth," said our one-eyed horse-wrangling genius, Areng. "It sounds like the bull of the local loose talk and of the big footprints."

Selby and I grunted. The longer one lives in Africa, the more one grunts. One grunts or one coos or one changes his voice from bass to falsetto to denote shadings of assent, dissent or skepticism—enthusiasm, despair, disbelief. We grunted skeptically. But you always run out your hits in Africa.

We jogged the nags to a little hill and climbed it just as the sun began to paint the stern blue mountains and the sere brown stretch of the scorched wasteland. Selby and Metheke had the glasses, and they began to search the terrain.

Metheke is a Wakamba gun bearer, and I have hunted with him for a dozen years. He is possibly the keenest sportsman I know, and above all he respects big elephants with big teeth. They scoured the land with the glasses, and suddenly both Africans—white Selby, black Metheke—began to coo.

They turned, beaming, twinlike despite the disparity of race and color, merged soulfully in true hunters' delight. They handed me the binoculars and pointed. Something filled the binoculars, and suddenly I began to coo too.

"Ah-ah-ah-ah-ah-ah-ah-*eeeee!*" I crooned, and almost fell off the boulder on which, apelike, I was perched in the crisp breeze of an early Kenya morning. Then we all slid down the hill and kicked the horses into a trot.

The old man was terribly, awfully old. He had lived too long—much too long. Quite possibly he had seen more than one century switch—the 18th change over to the 19th, the 19th to the 20th. Nobody will ever know accurately just how long a wild elephant lives. In zoos his life length is an average man's three-score-and-10 span. Twenty-one to grow up, 21 to fight and breed, 21 to teach his wisdom to the young bulls, and 10 or 20 more to brood and die. In Africa you would have to follow him on his many thousand miles of aimless meanderings from Ethiopia to Rhodesia to check him, to watch him grow huge and fight and breed and finally become outcast, and you would still never know if it was the same elephant if you had a hundred years to follow his plod. From the look of him, our old gentleman was at least 150 years old.

For many, many years he had been prison-pent. He had lived on this dry-river *luga* named Illaut. As long as the oldest native around the water hole could remember, he had lived near Illaut. He came to drink daily at the water hole a few hundred yards away from the only crap game in town—the one-room Somali general store, called *dukah* in East Africa. He was so far gone in ignobility that he no longer minded drinking with goats and donkeys. He did not even try to murder people anymore, because people and goats and sheep were really all he had to associate with.

The old bull was decades past his last breeding. He was long exiled from the world of other elephants. Likely one of his own sons had kicked him out. In any case, his memory of women and palm toddy was dim and possibly exaggerated. The young bulls no longer came to him for counsel, although his accumulated wisdom was vast. He had long since run through his repertoire of jokes and no longer found listeners for the chest-rumbling, trunk-probing, nostalgic tales of the good old days before the white man came with guns—the quiet days before the iron birds ripped the heavens apart with rude noise on their way to Ethiopia. Somehow the skies had been bluer in those days, and you could count on the seasons. Now the weather, like everything else, had gone bloody well mad. Three straight years of drought, for instance—and then it rained until it fair washed the country away, the Tana pouring red with eroded earth as it swept Kenya's lifeblood 40 miles out into the Indian Ocean.

He was more than a little deaf, of course, and certainly his eyesight was clouded by the years. His great ears, which once clapped like giant hands as he shook them irritably at the little hold-me-close flies or smacked thunderously against his head in harsh anger as he lofted his trunk and screamed in a charge, now hung in pathetic tatters; now his ears swung limp and shredded and flapped only feebly as he waved them. Over his entire back a green, mossy excrescence had grown. He was as barnacled as an old turtle or an ancient saltwater piling. He was wrinkled excessively, and perhaps he had lost three tons of weight from his original seven. He carried his tusks awkwardly as if they were too ponderous for his head, too heavy to tote in comfort now that all the counterbalancing weight had left his behind. How he'd reached this great age without breaking one or both tusks in this harsh, stone-studded country, with the full 30 years of routine fights, was one of God's mysteries. But there they were, great ivory parentheses stretching low and out and upward from his pendulous nether lip. Age had made him visually ridiculous; he wore a warrior's heavy weapons on his front end, and no single hair survived on his obscenely naked tail.

There would be curious growths in his belly that old elephants frequently have, like the hair balls one finds in the stomach of a crocodile or big catfish. Ants would have trammeled the length of his trunk; certainly his feet would be cracked and

149

wincing on the lava rocks of his self-imposed prison. You could tell this from the ridged tracks of his pad marks that covered 10 miles of country outside the water area. Old gentlemen's feet always hurt, and the pain is apt to make the owner tempery.

He swayed from side to side now and grumbled to himself, as old men will, and the burden of his complaint rode clear on the wind as we walked close—carelessly close— leaving the Somali ponies tethered to a thorn tree. The old bull had been a flashy traveling man in his time—all the way from the high blue hills of Ethiopia through Tanganyika and then into the Rhodesias, traversing the miles and miles of bloody Africa as he followed the dom palms whose red nuts he adored—as he occasionally ravished a maize field, as he whimsically butted over a railway train or upended a water tank or, just for the hell of it, swung his trunk like a rubbery scythe to wreck a native village. Cows had touched him tentatively with their trunks in girlish admiration; he had smelled the blood of a close cousin as he took out his tusks from a gut-spilling belly. Once sycophants had swarmed around him—young *askaris* eager for the knowledge he had amply to give; stooges to fetch and carry and always to heed his wit and his wisdom. All this the old man remembered.

Needed: more room for elephants. Where protected, they increase in number, overgraze their range, die of starvation.

But now he was very much all alone, chained by necessity to the creaking rocking chair of the limitations of old age. All the cows and calves and younger bulls were long gone. They had tolerated his presence in the area, even though he had become a bore with his stories of old slave caravans and regiments of spear-hunters. The country had played out. It had rained again on the other side of the mountain, and everybody had whistled off, following the fresh green that thrust upward under the rim of the escarpment. Everybody had gone but the old bull. He was too feeble to trek with them. His head was heavy, and his feet hurt.

Now he stood sadly alone, because he could not leave certain water for an uncertain excursion for food. And he was starving himself, because he had eaten the country clear. But he would not travel the usual two-day, 200-mile grazing distance of a younger bull. He had grazed his land rock-hard, and his tracks were imprinted atop each other. His dung abraded on itself in piles and was scattered by the passage of his own feet. He had made enough tracks for 200 elephants, and they were all his own.

Soon he would die. Unless the rains came almost immediately to green his prison yards he would die of senile decay and lack of nourishment—and, most of all, of purest boredom. The boredom was the worst of all the ills, and he would be glad to see the finish of it all.

There he stood now, pathetically magnificent on the slope of a sere brown rise, with the morning sun red behind him. There he stood against a cruel blue hill, his enormous curving tusks a monument to himself and to the Africa that was—the Africa that had changed, was changing, and would forevermore change until nothing beloved of it was left.

"Poor old beggar," the white hunter Selby said.

We had come there to shoot an elephant in an untouched, savage land, a land unmarked by tires, unseen by tourists. I did not weep when I shot the old bull twice through the heart and he crumpled to his creaking knees. In retrospect, yes, of course I would weep—but only as a respectful gesture to another age. When the old bull fell with a mighty crash, much of what I loved best of the old Africa died with him.

About the Illustrations

This book is a tribute to the illustrators whose work helped to make *The Saturday Evening Post* America's favorite magazine. In particular, it honors a number of artists who drew and painted animals superlatively well, with style and panache as well as technical virtuosity.

All of the pictures in this book appeared in the *Post* or in its companion publication, *The Country Gentleman*, between 1900 and 1941—before improved cameras and film made full-color animal photographs commonplace. The pictures reproduced here in two colors (usually red and black) were magazine covers prior to 1926 when new presses made full-color covers possible; the other colored pictures are

post-1926 magazine covers, while the smaller black and white pictures were story illustrations or page decorations that appeared at the beginnings or ends of articles.

Charles Livingston Bull, born in 1874, has been described as "half-naturalist, but all artist." He studied at the Philadelphia Art School but learned animal and bird anatomy at first hand, while becoming an expert taxidermist. Bull mounted a number of specimens for President Theodore Roosevelt and for the National Museum in Washington. After he became established as an artist, he traveled extensively in North and South America, observing wildlife in its native surroundings, and he lived for years opposite the Bronx Zoo so he could conveniently sketch from live animal models. Bull was an enthusiastic conservationist who banded birds for the U.S. Biological Survey and took an active role in early efforts to protect the American eagle from extinction.

Paul Bransom, born in 1885, learned drawing as an apprentice draftsman in the U.S. Patent Office at Washington; he learned about animals by spending all his free time observing and sketching at the National Zoo. For a time he drew a cartoon strip for a New York newspaper to earn a living while he continued studying and painting animals. In the course of a long and successful career, he illustrated some 50 books as well as hundreds of magazine articles and stories.

Other illustrators who specialized in portraying animals and whose work frequently appeared in the *Post* were Lynn Bogue Hunt and Jack Murray.

Still other artists are represented by examples of their work in this book because they painted birds and beasts along with people—often children—for the magazines. Among them: McClelland Barclay, L. Blumenthal, Franklin Booth, Harrison Fisher, George Gibbs, J. J. Gould, Elizabeth Shippen Green, E. M. Jackson, Oliver Kemp, Frank X. Leyendecker, J. C. Leyendecker, Emlen McConnell, Julius Moessel, Guernsey Moore, Peter Newell, Herman Pfeifer, Ellen Pyle, Norman Rockwell, Remington Schuyler, Henry J. Soulen, Leslie Thrasher, Gustave Verbeek and Sarah Stilwell Weber.

Acknowledgments

"The Bear" by William Faulkner Copyright 1942 and renewed 1970 by Estelle Faulkner and Jill Faulkner Summers. Reprinted by permission of Random House, Inc. An expanded version of this story appears in *Go Down, Moses* by William Faulkner.

"Columbus Saw It First" is reprinted by permission of Dodd, Mead & Co., Inc. from *Birds Over America* by Roger Tory Peterson. Copyright 1948, © 1964, 1976 by Roger Tory Peterson.

"The West was a Sea of Grass" is an excerpt from *The Generous Years: Remembrances of a Frontier Boyhood* by Chet Huntley Copyright © 1968 by Chet Huntley. Reprinted by permission of Random House, Inc.

"We Are Slow to Learn" is adapted from *America and the Americans* by John Steinbeck Copyright © 1966 by John Steinbeck. Reprinted by permission of Viking Press.

"The Woman Who Raised a Bear as Her Son" is reprinted by permission of Dodd, Mead & Co., Inc., from *The Day Tuk Became a Hunter* by Ronald Melzack. Copyright © 1968 by Ronald Melzack.

"Make Friends of Wild Animals" is an excerpt from *Wild Animals Around Your Home* by Paul Villiard Copyright © 1975 by Paul Villiard. Reprinted by permission of Winchester Press, 205 East 42nd Street, New York, N.Y. 10017.

"Build Bird Feeders and Houses" is adapted from *How to Attract, House and Feed Birds* by Walter E. Schutz.

Copyright © The Bruce Publishing Co. 1955, 1963, 1970. Used with permission of Macmillan Publishing Co., Inc.

"Lillian" ("Lillian of Broadway") by Damon Runyon is reprinted from *Guys and Dolls* by special arrangement with Sheldon Abend, Pres., The American Play Co., Inc., and Raoul L. Felder, Esq., 52 Vanderbilt Ave., New York, N.Y. 10017. Copyright © 1958 by Damon Runyon, Jr., and Mary Runyon McCann.

"Tom Edison's Shaggy Dog" is excerpted from the book *Welcome to the Monkey House* by Kurt Vonnegut, Jr. Copyright © 1953 by Kurt Vonnegut, Jr. Originally published in *Collier's*. Reprinted by permission of Delacorte Press/Seymour Lawrence.

"Josephine, the Tame Wild Boar" is from *The Animal World of Albert Schweitzer* Copyright 1950 by The Beacon Press. Reprinted by permission of the publisher.

"Rascal Makes Trouble" is excerpted from *Rascal* by Sterling North Copyright © 1963 by Sterling North. Reprinted by permission of the publishers, E. P. Dutton.

"My Last Safari" by Robert Ruark Copyright © 1963 by Robert Ruark. Reprinted by permission of the Harold Matson Co., Inc.

All illustrations in this book are reproduced from the pages of *The Saturday Evening Post* and *The Country Gentleman* and are the copyrighted property of The Curtis Publishing Company or The Saturday Evening Post Company.